WAITER & WAITRESS TRAINING

How to Develop Your Staff For Maximum Service & Profit

By Lora Arduser

D1024000

The Food Service Professional's Guide To:
Waiter & Waitress Training How to Develop Your
Staff For Maximum Service & Profit: 365 Secrets Revealed

Atlantic Publishing Group, Inc. Copyright © 2003
1210 SW 23rd Place
Ocala, Florida 34474
800-541-1336
352-622-5836 - Fax

www.atlantic-pub.com - Web Site
sales@atlantic-pub.com - E-mail

SAN Number :268-1250

International Standard Book Number: 0-910627-20-7

Library of Congress Cataloging-in-Publication Data

Arduser, Lora.
Waiter & waitress training : how to develop your staff for
maximum service & profit : 365 secrets revealed / by Lora
Arduser.
p. cm. -- (The food service professionals guide to ; 10)
ISBN 0-910627-20-7
1. Table service. 2. Waiters. 3. Waitresses. I. Title: Waiter
and waitress training. II. Title. III. Series.
TX925 .A73 2003
642'.6--dc21
20020137960

Printed in Canada

Book layout and design by Meg Buchner of Megadesign
www.mega-designs.com • e-mail: megadesn@mhtc.net

CONTENTS

Servers are the faces of your restaurant.

INTRODUCTION

Recently, a coworker asked his friend, "How was lunch?" The person replied, "The food was good, but the service was terrible!" This short exchange shows how important service is to your guests' dining experiences. Don't let someone leave your restaurant saying this!

Staff is one of your greatest assets as a restaurant owner and/or manager. Your employees have a tremendous influence on how profitable your establishment can be. Of course, how you hire and manage your employees is just as important.

While all your employees are an important part of the team, servers are particularly important because they are the faces of your restaurant. When customers dine in your establishment, at least 90 percent of their time is spent with their server. How your service caters to your guests is crucial in determining if they will be one-time customers – or repeat business. One-time customers obviously add to the bottom line, but your real profit potential lies in your repeat customers.

What can you do to make certain your servers are providing the customers with exceptional service? Read on! This book will show you how to hire, train, motivate and retain a great serving staff. As an added bonus, the principles can be applied to your entire staff. So, get reading and learn how to maximize the profits in your restaurant by developing your serving staff!

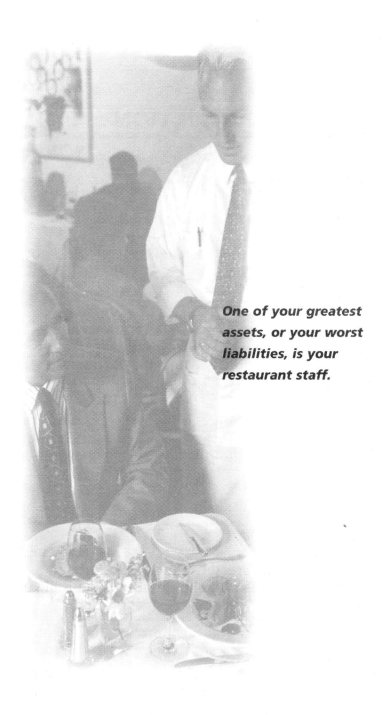

One of your greatest assets, or your worst liabilities, is your restaurant staff.

CHAPTER ONE

THE RESTAURANT TEAM

Who's Who? Your Serving Staff and Their Coworkers

One of your greatest assets, or your worst liabilities, is your restaurant staff. A good staff greatly affects your profit potential and a good staff doesn't just happen by accident. As a food service manager or owner, you have a tremendous impact on how good or bad your staff is. And, while this book focuses on how to develop your serving staff, a restaurant is a team and your servers can't do their jobs without the help of their coworkers. While all restaurants are different, most have the need for the same job roles:

Front-of-the-House

- **Greeter or host/hostess.** This person sets and keeps the tone of the restaurant because he or she is generally the first person the customer encounters. The host/greeter welcomes guests and assigns tables. If the greeter knows a guest's name, this information should always be relayed to the server. The greeter may also mention specials/options and should always set a pleasant tone for their dining experience. In addition, the host/greeter monitors current conditions for potential bottlenecks or problems and communicates among all team members, warns kitchen of crowd arrivals, alerts the manager to possible problems and performs any helpful chore, such as bussing, while traveling back and forth through the dining room.

- **Bartender.** If the establishment doesn't have a service bar, the bartender will intermingle with guests. The person can be aided, when busy, by a busser to fetch supplies, including garnishes from the kitchen, and to wash glasses.

- **Server.** The server is the main person that a customer will interact with in your restaurant. The server is responsible for serving guests and helping other servers when a need is noticed. Servers can use a rotating buddy system to provide flawless service to customers. They also may develop codes and signals to indicate when help is needed.

- **Busser.** The busser's main duty is to set up tables for customers and to clear tables. Set up entails wiping tables, placing silverware and water glasses and replacing candles or other tabletop decorations, as necessary. Bussers are often servers-in-training and they may cross-train at back-bar service. Bussers also often assist the dishwasher and may help the greeter.

Back-of-the-House

- **Kitchen staff.** Sometimes the chef is considered the most important member of staff in the entire food service business, but it is the smoothly functioning team, as a whole, that makes the dining experience a memorable one, bringing success to the establishment through repeat customers and increasing clientele. The chef's support crew (prep cook, salad prep, baker, etc.) is part of "the chef" when more than one person fills that function. The leader of the kitchen team is responsible for waste control, cost control and efficiency, as well as for implementing necessary safety and accident-prevention measures. The kitchen team is essentially an efficient "production line."

- **Dishwasher.** The dishwasher's main duties are to clean dishes and return them to the proper storage areas and to take care of trash. The rest of the staff can support dishwashers by separating silverware and glasses, disposing of broken dishes carefully and by clearing food from plates. Cross-training dishwashers can be useful, in case of the unexpected.

- **Management and administration.** The owner, the manager, or a team of people including cashier, accountant, purchasing clerk, parking valets, coat check person, etc., comprise this category. The manager should be visible and accessible, during busy hours, to both employees and guests and should act as a role model for the entire staff. The manager helps out wherever need exists. Good managers empower well-trained staff to handle most matters within guidelines, without needing to run for assistance. They also delegate management functions to staff that have the interest and capability to carry them out (safety, quality control, even marketing and promotion, etc.). They solve problems by involving everyone in the solution, from suggestions to execution. Also, they must always make sure that everyone understands why any particular decision was made or action was taken, especially if there have been differences of opinion on the subject.

Mission Statement

What is a mission statement? Your mission statement should tell you what your company's values are, who your customers are, what your economic objectives are, what your goals are, what your products are and what your market is. Here's how to develop a mission statement:

- **Components of a mission statement.** Your mission statement doesn't have to contain much detail at this stage; it is simply a device that will help you focus on your direction and begin formulating an idea of what type of restaurant you want to run. Take a sheet a paper with the following headings and write in the information:

  - Goals; e.g., to make a 15 percent profit or to establish an upscale breakfast restaurant.

  - Beliefs/Values; e.g., to provide quality food at affordable prices.

  - Product; e.g., the type of cuisine

  - Target customers; e.g., young working couples without children who have a good deal of disposable income.

  - Market; e.g., an urban center or a rural setting.

Goal Setting

Be sure to pay close attention to your goals. These need to be communicated to your staff on an ongoing basis so that they can keep these goals in focus as they are serving your customers, day in, day out. When setting goals, it is important to bear in mind, the following:

- **What are goals?** Goals are the performance targets that will accomplish your restaurant's mission. A goal may be to reduce waste, minimize cost or maximize serving efficiency.

- **Be specific.** Goals need to be clearly stated, specific and simple. Write goals down and amend when necessary.

- **Make sure your goals are realistic.** For example, if your labor cost has been running at 35 percent, don't expect to bring it down 15 percent in a single month.

- **Goals must be measurable and consistent.** It is easier to reach a goal of cutting operating costs by 2 percent rather than simply cutting operation costs.

- **Involve your staff.** Finally, and perhaps most importantly, be sure to explain how each staff member can contribute to achieving your overall mission and individual goals.

You as the Leader

As the restaurant owner and/or manager, you are the leader of your team of employees. Here are some tips that will help you to become a successful leader:

- **Leadership qualities.** What makes a good leader?

Think back to bosses you had during your early years in the food service industry. Who stands out and why? You probably remember the managers that respected employees, showed concern for their staff and were not afraid to pitch in wherever needed. These are all qualities that make a good leader.

- **Do as I say and as I do.** If you don't want your staff to hang round the back booth chatting when business is slow, don't engage in this activity yourself! Show them how you want them to act as well as telling them. If management doesn't show concern for how the customer is treated, then employees are unlikely to perform any better.

- **During the dinner and/or lunch rushes be sure to be on the floor.** As you walk through the dining room, if you see a plate that a customer has finished with, bus it. If water glasses need refilling, refill them! You'll show your servers that you care about the customer enough to do these things and they'll emulate your behavior.

- **Know yourself.** Know your own strengths and weaknesses; capitalize on the former and minimize the latter. If you have poor math skills, hire an accountant to compensate for this weakness. If your people skills are strong, make sure you spend a lot of time on the floor with your employees and customers.

- **Be part of the team.** Pitch in when someone is missing. Your employees will appreciate your effort and respect you for lending a hand rather than managing "from on high."

- **Always remember that your employees are individuals.** Accept the different styles of your employees, but always expect good performance, as well. Be alert to the training and development needs of each individual employee. Meet those needs.

- **Be fair and consistent with policies and procedures.** Treat all your employees equally. Don't show favoritism. If you dock one employee's pay for an unexcused absence, don't look the other way when the next employee is a no show with no excuse.

- **Reinforce positive behavior.** The saying "you catch more flies with honey" is true. You are more likely to get the behavior you want out of your employees if you reward them for acceptable behavior. While you always have to discipline for inappropriate behavior, let someone else know they did a good job and that you appreciate it.

- **Help your employees relate to the bigger picture.** Employees can easily get bogged down by detail and focus on one dish or one table, to the detriment of the rest of their duties. It can be difficult for them to step back and see how their behavior might affect the business and profits as a whole. Point out the benefits of good service: happier customers and more income for both the restaurant and themselves.

- **Encourage.** Make an effort to encourage your staff to communicate with each other and yourself. Let them know that you want to know what they need and what they appreciate. By understanding their needs, you'll make working together much easier!

- **Be careful not to assemble a team of "yes men."** Creative solutions to problems come from diverse points of view, so don't surround yourself with other management team members who think just like you do. Encourage those who disagree to speak up as well. You may, for example, want to consider rotating meeting leadership to make sure your own point of view isn't the only one heard all the time. Here are some danger signs that you are surrounded by "yes men":
    - They look to you to start or end the discussions and meetings.

    - They address you more formally than others.

    - They don't speak spontaneously without asking permission.

    - They don't disagree or question your opinions.

    - They look to you as judge.

    - They don't confront each other for impeding progress, without waiting for you to take the lead.

- **Be creative when looking for solutions.** In meetings, when you are looking for solutions, state your target/problem simply and clearly. Often, solutions are to be found within a range of possibilities with no single answer being right. Begin by brainstorming and appoint one or two "recorders" to keep track of all ideas. Halfway through, change recorders and also freshen the mix of the group. Encourage people to "play" and enjoy using their imaginations. Last of all, consider the suggestions logically and inventively.

- **Dealing with conflicts.** Conflict resolution is a tricky part of being a leader. Remember, conflict is not always a negative thing and can often be useful. Encourage people to speak up about what bothers them. Engage in active listening when dealing with a conflict. Also be sure to set norms for politeness, good behavior and honesty.

Teamwork

While you may be the leader in your food service organization, you can't do everything. Consideration for one's colleagues and cooperation create a more productive environment, especially when circumstances are particularly demanding. Working and thinking as a team helps to create an environment of collaboration, which will help to ensure your restaurant's ability to make profits. Teamwork can increase your productivity, improve decision making, maximize the use of your human resources and make better use of your inventory. Make problem solving an automatic function of daily work, by team training. Customer service also benefits from smooth teamwork. You can improve the bottom line – profitability – by efficient team building:

- **What is a team?** A team is a manageable number of people with similar or coordinated functions working together for the common goal of providing seamless service. Usually 2-25 people (ideally 10-15 people) make a manageable team. You can think of teams as front-of-the-house teams and back-of-the-house teams. If you have a large staff, one particular position could be a team, or your teams could be organized by shift.

- **Team members' characteristics.** The members of a team must have common goals, similar or complementary functions and equal responsibility for team performance. Everyone should have the same definitions of "team" and "teamwork" for the teams to be successful.

- **Choosing team leaders.** To delegate some responsibility, choose team leaders. These people do not necessarily have to be the best performers, but they should be people who can motivate and train others and carry a full load. They will be the "naturals," the ones to whom others naturally look. Make sure you have more than one leader for each team so that changing schedules can be accommodated and no shift will be without a team leader.

- **Functions of team leaders.** In many ways, team leaders function as management. Team leaders should hold the team together and define individual member roles. They also guide and train team members. They also ensure open communication among team members and solicit solutions from within the team. Other functions team leaders can fulfill include monitoring performance, providing feedback, working as a liaison to other team leaders and communicating and demonstrating that team success is the responsibility of each individual on the team. Team leaders can also act as spokespersons for presenting problems or ideas to management.

- **Train team leaders first.** You can let them train team members and this can become part of your restaurant's overall training program.

- **Team building.** Be sure to engage in team-building behavior. A team falls apart easily if you fail to reinforce the fact that they are a team working for a common goal. Let members get to know each other in a casual setting. Perhaps have a staff party, take instant photos of teams and put them on bulletin boards in the back of the facility. You could also create a scrapbook that includes personal details, pets, family and personal goals. Update it regularly.

- **Individual accountability** within team accountability. If one member of a team doesn't perform, the whole team suffers and team trust is compromised. Be sure to reward good behavior, but also set conditions for poor behavior and make sure everyone knows the standards. It is not useful simply to say, "Don't make mistakes" or "Don't have accidents." Find out why an employee is having problems and work together to find the cause and a solution.

- **Don't demand perfection from your servers.** It will only lead to hiding mistakes and undermining the team, as well as the establishment.

- **Not all teams are the same.** Kitchen team members are more specialized and less likely to switch functions. Front team members have primary, but not fixed, responsibilities and are more likely to interchange functions, covering for each other for smooth service. Make sure all team members understand the differences and what their own responsibilities are.

- **Cross-training the front-of-the-house.** A slowdown in one function can upset the entire flow of service to all customers. The team leader can define and assign secondary task responsibilities, during the daily meeting. Sometimes a buddy system works well to adjust front-of-the-house staff to shift away from the "not-my-job" syndrome. The server who is tipped according to service performance is affected in the long run by someone else's temporary work buildup. If the same server has regular trouble, then consider additional training. Include answering the phone as one function that may need coverage.

- **Teamwork training.** There are online sources available to help train your management and staff in teamwork. For training materials and information on teamwork training, visit:
  - www.conferencecontent.com/content_team-building.htm

  - www.facilitationfactory.com/interstitial.html

  - www.temeculacreek.com/ball.htm

  - www.corvision.com/teams.htm

Scheduling

In order to make your restaurant profitable and keep within your budgets, you must keep your labor costs under control. How you schedule labor will have a major impact on labor costs. Here are some important guidelines:

- **Determining labor cost for a shift.** Once you've written out the schedule for a particular shift, multiply the hours worked by each employee by their hourly wage. Now, project what your sales will be for that shift and divide it by the number you came up with for the labor cost for the shift. This will give you a labor percentage. Is this figure acceptable from a profit standpoint? If not, you may want to make some adjustments to your scheduling.

- **Consider letting team leaders do their own scheduling.** Team interaction is good for team spirit. By having leaders schedule their team's hours, you can encourage this interaction – and have someone to help you with the headaches of scheduling! Make sure team leaders let shifts overlap by a few minutes, so as to ease the turnover from one group to the next. It also makes it easier to keep track of requested vacation time and other predictable time off, so you can prepare your requirement listings ahead of time.

- **Helpful hints.** Whether you or team leaders do the scheduling, keep the following in mind:
  - Try to schedule one day off each week, preferably two, for each employee.

  - Watch for burnout from over-scheduling.

  - Have alternates tagged in case of last-minute emergencies.

  - Make sure to have at least one team leader on each shift.

- **Scheduling software.** Employee Schedule Partner is a complete software package for employee scheduling. Just point and click to create a schedule, without touching the keyboard. Click a button and the software will automatically fill your schedule with employees. Click a button to replace absent employees and a list of available employees and phone numbers will appear. The online coach provides helpful hints for new users. The package accommodates an unlimited number of employees and positions. You can manually override selections at any time and track employees' availability restrictions. Schedule employees to work multiple shifts per day. Track payroll and hourly schedule totals for easy budget management. Schedules can begin on any day of the week. Track stations as well as positions. Specify maximum hours per day, days per week and shifts per day for each employee. Lock any employee into a scheduled shift so the program will not move them when juggling the schedule. Save old schedules for reference when needed. The software is even password protected to prevent unauthorized use. Employee Schedule Partner is available from Atlantic Publishing Company, www.atlantic-pub.com, 800-541-1336; Item ESP-CS.

- **Employee Time Clock Partner.** This is a complete employee time clock software package. It is very powerful yet simple to use. Automatically clock in and out (just enter your employee number and you are clocked in or out). Employees can view their time cards to verify information. It is password protected so only management may edit time card information. It even calculates overtime both daily and weekly. Management can assign employee ID numbers or PINs (personal identification numbers). Employee Time Clock Partner is available from Atlantic Publishing Company, www.atlantic-pub.com, 800-541-1336; Item ETC-CS.

Train Management First

Before you start to train your waitstaff, make sure that your management and team leaders are properly trained. Many people in restaurant management positions are promoted through the ranks and many of these people have no management experience whatsoever. Get them that training so that they can manage the rest of the staff, effectively. If you don't, you'll start seeing problems, such as turnover and sloppy work. Consider the following training possibilities:

- **Training resources.** For a complete range of training resources, including books, videos, software and posters, see www.atlantic-pub.com.

- **Hospitality management courses.** Check with your area colleges and vocational schools. Many have hospitality management programs. It would be wise to enroll your new managers on one of these programs.

- **Online courses.** The number of online options available to the restaurant industry is growing. Check out the following Web sites for distance learning courses that could be useful to your managers:
    - Cornell University School of Hotel Administration. Online courses include Managing People More Effectively and other courses in hospitality marketing, management of hospitality human resources and hospitality accounting. You can register online at www.ecornell.com or over the phone at 866-ecornell (866-326-7635).

- The American Hotel and Lodging Educational Institute also offers many hospitality and management courses online at www.ei-ahla.org/offsite.asp?loc=www.ahma.com.

- The Culinary Institute of America has recently introduced online courses at www.ciaprochef.com.

- Atlantic Publishing offers ServSafe® management certification programs and courses at www.atlantic-pub.com.

Role of Communication in Managing Your Staff

Communication between you and your serving staff is just as important as the communication between your servers and your customers. Try the following approach:

- **Engage in active listening.** How many times have you caught yourself daydreaming or planning when you were supposed to be listening to someone? It happens to us all at times. When communicating with your staff, however, you want to engage in active listening. Make sure they know that you've heard them. As you are listening, nod, lean forward and maintain eye contact. Using short verbalizations such as "I see" or "uh huh" lets the person know you're actively following them. Verify that you understand, by repeating. You can say "I hear you saying ..." or "You seem disturbed by..."

- **Eliminate negative speaking.** The words we choose have a major impact on how people hear what we are saying. Replace phrases such as "I can't," "I should have," and "What's wrong with" with phrases like "I haven't yet," "Starting now, I will," and "How can we improve?"

- **Overcome cultural barriers and achieve diversity.** The restaurant industry has a very diverse employment base. Teach yourself and other employees tolerance and show respect for all race, gender, sexual preference and religious differences. If you have a bilingual staff, you should also provide language assistance, including English for foreign speakers and foreign words/phrases for English speakers. See www.atlantic-pub.com for simple food service guidebooks. There are many sources for bilingual training. Berlitz Languages Centers can provide group training. For the center nearest you, call 800-457-7958, or log on to www.berlitz.com. Language Learning Enterprises also offers tutoring and training. They can be reached at www.lle-inc.com. The National Association for Bilingual Education tracks federal policies that can help employers. You can reach them at www.nabe.org. Worldwide Language Center is another training resource that can tailor instruction to a restaurant environment. Call them at 703-527-8666, or log on to www.worldwide.edu. You also might check with area colleges. Also, you may be able to find a college graduate student willing to take on a freelance project. For cultural diversity training products, visit HR Press's Web site at www.hrpress-diversity.com.

- **Watch interactions amongst staff to identify those being excluded.** Ask those excluded what they feel would make them become part of the team. A good way to include loners is to get mixed groups together for "games" and coach them, and involve all employees in decisions.

Building Trust and Team Spirit

Ask the dishwasher what he does. If he replies, "I wash dishes," you've some work to do. If he replies "I make sure that the restaurant can function properly by providing a constant supply of clean dishes," then, you've succeeded. Every person in the organization is important and has a critical role. Ensure that employees know their roles in your organization. In order to get the best from your team, you need to build trust. Here's how:

- **Levels of trust.** When working in a team environment, there are three levels of trust:
  - High: "I'm not concerned because I'm certain that others will not take advantage of me."

  - Low: "I need to see that I get my fair share and others don't take too much."

  - None: "I'll get them before they get me."

- **You can build trust many different ways.** Try spending social time together. Make some jobs two-person jobs (e.g., cleaning, napkin folding, etc). Encourage discussion of problems and issues and let staff know that asking for help is okay. Improve communication and eliminate fear of ridicule or reprisal. Make room for the personal – "I feel," "I think," "What do you feel about...?" Provide positive reinforcement for helpful behavior and allow time for trust to grow.

- **Banish untrusting behaviors.** Make sure that no one on your staff or management team engages in the following behavior:
  - Ignoring people

- Embarrassing someone in front of others
- Failing to keep confidences
- Avoiding eye contact
- Withholding credit where due
- Interrupting others
- Not helping when able
- Taking over for someone who doesn't need help
- Breaking a promise

- **Lead by challenge and positive reinforcement.**
  Set goals just ahead of expectations and reward
  employees when goals are reached. Try using
  scoreboards: 102 days since last accident, 2,453
  meals served, 1,134 orders – no mistakes, etc.
  Continually set new goals, but don't make goals
  too hard to achieve. Be sure that people
  understand the targets you have set for them.
  People feel secure in knowing what is expected.

- **Recognize, reinforce and compensate
  outstanding performance.** Recognition by itself is
  reinforcement and may not need compensation. A
  specific and timely "well done" often holds as
  much weight as monetary compensation, but
  monetary rewards have their place as well. Have a
  ready supply of movie passes and other "goodies"
  to distribute to the deserving. Even keep some in
  your pocket for any meritorious action you just
  happen to see in passing. Match the size of the
  reward to the size of the performance accomplish-
  ment. Have an annual "Academy Awards"
  ceremony with categories suited to your business
  (Biggest Helping Hand, Most Infectious Smile, Most
  Improved Performance, etc.). Make it a big deal
  with invitations and a special menu. Let each
  employee bring guests. Set up a committee to
  select the winners.

- **Sales incentives.** Start with the end result in mind and work backwards. Communicate specifically. For instance, tell your staff you are looking for a particular percentage increase in dollar sales of some item, such as desserts. Break that down into how many desserts per day, per shift and per person need to be sold and be sure that is a manageable goal for each team member. Remember, this is not a quota, but a goal for the team. It allows for more than one "winner" while the whole team wins. This may also provide an opportunity to motivate the "slower" employees back into peak performance. Everyone should be in on both planning and carrying out incentives and the reward system for goals accomplished. Some rewards for good work include money, recognition, time off, a "piece of the action," getting favored assignments, promotion or advancement, freedom, personal growth, having fun and prizes.

Low- and No-Cost Employee Motivational Programs

What most motivates the people who work in your restaurant is recognition, not money! You don't need to spend a lot of money (or any at all) to let employees know how much you appreciate their efforts. What are the best ways to reward your employees for superior performance? Recognition by management, money, time off, advancement, promotion, prizes and gifts. Here are some great ideas:

- **Treat your top performing employees the best!** Create and foster an atmosphere of "employees who do the best, receive the most rewards"! Positive reinforcement of top performers will return even greater performance.

- **Eliminate "but" from your vocabulary.** Whether you are counseling an employee, giving them a pat on the back, or a combination (You are doing great, but...). Your employee will forget everything positive before the BUT and will only remember the negative that comes after this.

- **Focus on the top.** Don't spend 85 percent of your time giving extra time and attention to the bottom performers, while all but ignoring your top performers. They may tend to feel the lack of attention is due to their performance and may – negatively – alter their work habits. Concentrate on your mid- to upper-level performers. Encourage their growth and development. The bottom performers will likely go elsewhere.

- **Cut loose your sea anchor!** A sea anchor is a nautical term for a sail that is dragged behind a vessel in the water to slow down or stop forward movement. While this principle worked great in sailing years, the notion of carrying dead weight will slow or drag down even the best organization, and ultimately cost you profits and employees. Cut the anchor loose!

- **Try to avoid cash awards.** Sounds crazy, but think of it this way: Cash awards go directly into a paycheck. Most employees don't share this information with coworkers. Instead, present gift certificates in your company (returning the business to your company) and present them with a plaque or other award. A plaque on a wall is a constant reminder to the employee and others that you recognize top performance.

- **Challenge employees!** Even the best employees

need to be challenged. Don't settle for the same performance, same tasks, day in and day out. Challenging employees does two things: it builds confidence and better employee satisfaction as they accomplish more difficult tasks, and it develops future leaders for your organization by challenging them beyond normal levels.

- **If you insist on cash rewards, specify the terms.** A great example is an incentive program that rewards employees with cash assistance to purchase a computer. This small reward will pay dividends for years, by allowing employees additional training on computer usage (during their own time). It also serves as a constant reminder of what the company did for them! This builds loyalty and ultimately enhances performance.

- **Develop non-cash-related rewards programs.** Some may include:
  - Suggestion programs (to reduce costs)
  - Employee of the month
  - Timeliness rewards
  - Rewards for working extra shifts
  - Successfully completing training programs
  - Free movie tickets
  - Thank-you letters/thank-you e-mails
  - Designated parking spot
  - Free merchandise; e.g., T-shirt with your logo

- **Develop more cash-related rewards programs.** Some may include:
  - Free dinners
  - Free gas, oil and lube change certificate
  - Time off

- Gift certificate (home improvement, electronics, books)

- **Idea incentive program.** Safety program (identify/remove safety hazards – how much does an accident cost you?)

- **Loyalty incentives** (one year of employment, two years, etc...)

- **Rewards for guest comments and surveys** (perks programs - three positive comments = four hours off!)

- **Personalize gifts.** Take the time to write a hand-written congratulatory note. This goes a long way in comparison with the computer-generated thank-you note your secretary types! Personalize plaques with their names and even their photos, etc.

- **Informal awards/recognition programs.** "On-the-spot" awards. The idea is that you don't have to take it to vote, to the board, to the awards committee, etc. Empower management to give out on-the-spot awards (small bonuses, time off, etc.). Employees know managers have this power and will rise to the occasion to earn the rewards for their hard work.

- **"Pat-on-the-back" awards.** These are the kinds of awards that cost nothing – and usually return the best results. "Pat-on-the-back" awards are just that; quick, informal and certainly appreciated by employees. A perfect example is telling the kitchen staff that the meal they prepared was delicious. That is true job satisfaction!

- **Pins and button rewards.** Pins, buttons and other trinkets for the employee to wear, proudly. Employee of the Month, Best Overall, Best Smile, etc., are low-cost, but high return in satisfaction, plus your employee shares the award with everyone with whom he or she comes into contact.

- **Group activities.** Morale Day cookouts, barbecues, beer-bashes, etc. Make it during the normal workday for a double bonus – time off and a great party. This has several benefits: it shows you care, it allows management to socialize with employees and gives you an opportunity to bond (prove you are human too!).

- **Showcase employees.** Have you seen those Wal-Mart commercials featuring Wal-Mart employees? Yes, those employees are real – they appear as a reward for superior performance.

- **Recognize your people in public.** Recognition behind closed doors loses the power of the presentation – an audience remembers recognition!

CHAPTER TWO

ELEMENTS OF SERVICE

Pet Peeves

Results from *Food and Wine's* Food in America 2002 survey clearly indicate to any restaurant owner/manager that customers consider service to be an important part of their overall dining experience. Findings from the survey include the following diner pet peeves:

Waitstaff that disappears 23%
Vain/snotty waitstaff 13%
Waitstaff that hovers 5%
Long waits between courses...........................5%
Specials given without prices 2%

- **Food is why a customer chooses a restaurant, but service is a major reason why guests come back.** Good service begins with employees' knowledge of the restaurant's concept, menu, wine and their ability to share that knowledge with the customer, but it encompasses many other factors as well.

Service Delivery Systems

You need to define what kind of service you have at your restaurant before you can define the elements that constitute good service. Here is a list of the possible types of service. There are advantages and disadvantages to all. Which one fits your restaurant?

- **French.** French service is very formal and the food is cooked or completed at a side table, in front of the customer. Common applications, in American restaurants, include preparing Crepes Suzettes or Bananas Foster. In French service, two people serve a table. The advantage of French service is that the customer gets a great deal of attention. The disadvantage is that it takes a highly skilled staff and is time-consuming. To upgrade your service, you may want to consider preparing some desserts or salads tableside.

- **Russian.** Russian service is as formal as French service. The main difference between the two is that with Russian service, the food is prepared in the kitchen and served to the guest from platters rather than on a plate. Also, Russian service only requires one server. It is faster than French service, but there is the added expense of platters and serving utensils.

- **English.** In English service, the food is brought from the kitchen on platters and set before the host or the person at the head of the table. This style of service is often used for a dinner in a private room of a restaurant rather than for the usual restaurant service. The host plates the dinners and hands them to the server to pass to all the guests. This style of service requires a lot of work and can be time-consuming. It does make a nice show, however, for special occasions.

- **American.** American service is less formal than the three previously discussed styles and is the type of service found in most American restaurants. Basically, food is prepared and plated on individual plates in the kitchen, then brought out to the guests.

- **Buffet.** Buffet service refers to a type of service in which guests pick up their plates, then fill them from items set out on long tables in the dining area. This is the type of serve at most weddings and other private events. Some restaurants, such as Old Country Buffet, use this as their main style of service. However, some restaurants use it as part of their service. Many establishments have a salad or breakfast bar that works the same way.

- **Counter.** Counter service is the type of service seen in fast-food restaurants. The advantage of counter service is the speed at which you can serve the customer. The disadvantage is that the customer receives little attention. If you want to increase your sales by offering service that is faster than your normal service, consider offering carryout or delivery.

Left or Right?

Food service literature suggests that there is little agreement on the correct sides from which food should be served. However, there is a general consensus of opinion regarding certain points of service that all waitstaff should know. One main rule servers can follow is that women are generally waited on before the men. Use the following serving suggestions as a guide:

- **Appetizers and salads.** Appetizers and salads should be served from the right with the right hand. The flatware for appetizers and salads is usually already on the table.

- **Soups.** If soup is being served, make sure the bowl is on a plate. Add a nice touch, with a doily underneath the bowl. Soup spoons should be set to the right of the bowl and soup served from the right.

- **Entrée.** Entrées are also served from the right. It should be placed so the main element of the plate faces the guest. Flatware for the entrée should be placed on the table before the entrée arrives. Be sure the servers only touch the flatware by the handle and plates by the rim. If side dishes are served on separate plates, they should be served from the left.

- **Dessert.** When serving dessert, the waitperson should place the utensil to the guest's left and serve the dessert from the right.

- **Beverages.** Drinks are served from the right and coffee is poured from the right.

- **Clearing.** In general, all plates and other dishes should be cleared from the right.

- **Signs that a guest is done.** These signals include placing a napkin on top of the plate, pushing the plate to the side and turning the fork upside down across the plate, or both the knife and fork placed together, at an angle on the plate. However, even if your server sees these signals at a table, he or she should first ask the guests before they clear.

- **Resources.** For more information on serving etiquette, visit CuisineNet digest's Web site at www.cuisinenet.com/digest/custom/etiquette/serving.shtm and Western Silver's site at www.terryneal.com/manners1.htm. For wine serving etiquette, visit Tasting Wine at www.tasting-wine.com/html/etiquette.html. You can find answers to etiquette and serving questions at the Online Manners Guy site at www.terryneal.com/manners1.htm.

Knowing What Your Customers Want

Obviously, your customers want good food and good service. They also want reasonable prices. In order for your servers to deliver exceptional service, they (and you) need to know more specifically what your customer wants. Does your typical customer want to be pampered or left alone? Do they tend to want a fast meal or a leisurely paced meal? Do they want haute cuisine or simple fare? Take a look at the following sources of information:

- **Industry research.** Industry research can help you come up with your customer profile. It can also help you figure out what type of dining experience your customers are after. Some online sources for industry information include:
  - Gallup Poll at www.gallup.com

  - The Nation's Restaurant News' research page at www.nrnresearch.com/NRNResearchHome.asp

  - The National Restaurant Association's Web site at www.restaurant.org

- Consumer Reports on Eating-Out Share Trends (CREST) at www.npd.com

- Restaurant USA's Web site at www.restaurant.org/rusa/magArticle.cfm?Articl eID=765

- The U.S. Department of Labor's Bureau of Labor Statistics' Consumer Expenditure Survey at www.bls.gov/cex lists results from surveys the bureau conducts of households in which every household member keeps a list of all their expenditures. This annual survey can give you information on how much money consumers spend on food away from home.

- *Restaurants and Institutions'* Red Zone Survey at www.rimag.com is a questionnaire dealing with meals purchased outside the home. Questions include when and where people ate, how they made their dining decision, how much they spent and what they ate.

- **Customer surveys.** Customer surveys don't have to be elaborate and they can give you a great deal of knowledge about what your customers want. You can have servers give customers a survey at the end or their meal, or you may want to have a suggestion box that allows customers to give you feedback (anonymously) on your service.

- **Menu sales mix.** Looking at your menu sales will tell you about your guests' tastes in the past and how these tastes are changing. Look at your menu sales from last year and compare to last week. What are the hot sellers? When were you busy and when did you have slow periods?

- **Talk to your servers.** Servers are the main point of contact for your customers. Talk with them to find out if customers are happy about the new dining room décor or if the new appetizer menu just isn't going over very well.

- **Personal observation.** Use your own observation skills. You're in the dining room everyday; what do you see your customers "ooohing" and "aahing" over? What puts a sour look on your customers' faces? Also, use your personal experience of dining at other restaurants. What really made a meal for you? As a diner, what are your pet peeves?

What Makes a Good Server?

Servers are essentially internal marketing tools. They are the link between your customers and sales, so you want a server who is going to be successful at marketing your menu and establishment to their guests. Obviously, knowledge and experience make a person a good server, but what character traits should you look for in an individual that will tell you they would shine as a server? Here are some guidelines:

- **Effective communicator.** One of a server's main jobs is to communicate with customers and the rest of your staff. Servers should be able to communicate with a wide range of personalities. This communication extends to facial expressions and body language. If a server is frowning at a guest, he or she is communicating negative emotions, whereas a natural smile implies a welcoming emotion.

- **High energy.** Restaurant serving is a tough job

that requires many hours of walking and long periods on your feet. Servers need to be able to maintain this energy level throughout a shift.

- **Flexibility.** Servers should be flexible and able to deal with sudden, unexpected rushes that require them to extend their shift. They also need to be flexible and tolerant in dealing with the public.

- **Can handle stress.** The restaurant world is a stressful one and servers will have to deal with physical and mental stress on a daily basis. This stress can take the form of annoying customers, a surly kitchen crew, another server that won't pull his or her own weight, or simply dealing with a full restaurant.

- **Cooperative.** Restaurants require a good deal of teamwork and cooperation. Therefore, servers should be willing to pitch in and help. For example, a good server would help the salad person when he or she was backed up; a less-than-ideal server would stand and wait for his or her salads, with hands on hips.

- **Courteous.** Servers should be polite and courteous with their managers, fellow employees and guests. There are no "ifs," "ands" or "buts" about it!

- **Desire to please others.** The job of server is aptly named. A person that is working in such a position should get satisfaction from pleasing other people. A server must be able to put his or her ego in check for the good of the customer, as well as for the good of the tip!

- **Empathic.** Good servers can read a customer

quickly and see if they want to be alone or are interested in chatting. This ability to feel and reflect another person's mood is helpful for setting the right tone for a guest. If a solitary diner is reading, the server shouldn't loiter, automatically assuming the person is lonely. If the guest encourages conversation, that's fine, otherwise, he or she may simply be interested in the book they've brought along!

- **Neat appearance.** Servers need to be neat and clean. Your server indicates to your guest how clean and organized your facility is. If the server runs up to the table frantically searching for a pen, wearing a dirty apron and shirt, the customer is going to feel that this reflects how much you care about the rest of your operation.

Before the Customers Arrive

Servers have many responsibilities, prior to the arrival of guests. Before they start their work, they must be assigned stations for the shift. You should try to make these stations as evenly distributed as possible. Unfortunately, all stations are not equal. Some are better than others, so have a policy to rotate servers through the different stations. You may want to base this policy on seniority or sales, or you may prefer to do a simple, unbiased rotation. Also, consider the following server responsibilities:

- **Setting up the tables.** Before the front doors open, servers need to make sure that all the tables in their stations are ready for guests. Wipe all the tables off or check linen tablecloths to make sure they're spotlessly clean. Also check the seats and floor under the table for crumbs or stickiness. Check to make sure that the condiment containers are full and that all decorations look attractive. If there are fresh flowers, make sure they are still fresh. If candles look used, change them. Bus people help with these tasks through the shift, but the server should be responsible for seeing that setups are complete, at the beginning and the end of the shift.

- **Napkins, silverware and glassware.** After checking the tables, servers should prepare the flatware and napkins. If you own a fine-dining establishment, you may have certain napkin folds the servers must create. Be sure the servers check all flatware, wine glasses and water glasses for cleanliness, before placing them on the table! For resources on napkin folding, check out the following books: *The Simple Art of Napkin Folding: 94 Fancy Folds for Every Tabletop Occasion* by Linda Hetzer; *Simply Elegant Napkin Folding* by Chris Jordan, or *Beautiful Napkin Folding* by Horst Hanisch. These books are available online at www.atlantic-pub.com, or check with your local bookseller or library.

- **Prepare the back area.** After the tables are set, servers should prepare their communal area. They will need to make coffee and iced tea, prefill water pitchers, cut lemons, stock sugar and cream, prepare bread baskets, gather guest checks and check the stock of children's menus and place mats.

- **Check the menu and specials.** The servers should also check the menu and the specials for that day. If you have a board where you write the specials, make sure the servers get into the habit of checking it and asking any questions, before they serve their first customer. It's also a good idea for servers to review the menu before serving to refresh their memories. This is especially important if you employ part-time servers. It's easy for people who only work a few times a week to forget the details.

- **Closing.** To close the dining room after the shift, your servers should essentially do what they did when they came in. They should reset all the tables and restock any items they can for the next shift. If it's an evening shift, also make sure they turn off any equipment that needs to be shut down.

How to Provide Great Service

Great service doesn't just happen by accident. There are many things your servers and you can do to give your customers exceptional service. Consider the following opportunities:

- **Smile.** This is one of the simplest yet most important things your servers (and management) can do. Smiling sets the tone and sets everyone at ease; it makes the server approachable for the customer. If the staff is unsmiling and surly, customers may never return to your establishment.

- **Servers stay with diners.** In many restaurants today, managers use multiple employees to wait on a table. While this results in speedy delivery, it can also confuse the guest. Give your servers the opportunity to connect to the guest; let them be the sole liaison between restaurant and guest. Of course, this doesn't mean that no one should help the server if she or he is behind.

- **Maintain a database.** Keep a record of your regular customers' likes, dislikes, birthdays, anniversaries, etc. Nothing makes a customer feel more special than having his or her birthday remembered – without even prompting! Use your computer system to develop such a database, or simply keep a notebook. Many restaurants have POS systems that capture information such as birthdays, anniversaries, etc. If you don't have such a system, create your own. You can capture the information though customer surveys. Give this information to the host/hostess. Include people's names and what particular guests like to drink. Also, inform servers about forthcoming, special occasions.

- **Guest book.** Make sure your guests fill in the guest book; you need a mailing list of your patrons for sending them promotional material. Try to collect birth dates and anniversaries for your database as well.

- **Recognition.** Recognition is very important, but it doesn't necessarily need to be elaborate. It can be as simple as addressing the customer by name.

- **Listen carefully for information from customers.** Better to overcommunicate than to drop the ball. Servers may want to repeat information back to customers, especially if the order is detailed. This will let the guest know the server wrote it down correctly. If your restaurant doesn't use guest checks when taking the customer's order at the table, this device can be particularly important for reassuring the customer.

- **Make eye contact.** As a culture, Americans tend to trust people who look you in the eye. Look directly at the customer you are addressing. Give your guests your undivided attention and let them know that you are listening. Don't stare at the table, the floor or the artwork on the wall. Clear your head, smile and pay attention. Make sure you're at the table when you're talking. Don't talk to your guests as you're flying by. It makes people feel unimportant, and no one likes that feeling.

- **Use an expediter.** An expediter is someone who maintains the pace in the kitchen. This person keeps track of the food coming out of the kitchen and makes sure servers know where their plates are and what needs to go out to the dining room next. This person can be key in making sure service is smooth and timely. You don't necessarily need to hire someone just for this position. If your seasoned veterans would like more hours, have them fill this position on a rotating basis.

- **Create shorthand codes.** All restaurants use shorthand on their guest checks to communicate information. It's simply quicker than writing everything out. Make sure your servers are well acquainted with the appropriate codes. It can be disastrous if they start to make up their own!

- **Rules of the road.** Have set traffic rules in your establishment. Make sure that aisles don't become clogged. For example, if two servers are heading for the same table, the first one should go to farthest side of the table. Always let the guest go first, then a server with food and finally the busser.

- **Rules of recovery.** Accidents are bound to happen; how you handle the accident is the important thing. First, promptly offer an honest, sincere apology. Second, take steps to resolve the problem. Let's say one of your servers spills tomato bisque on the white shirt of one of your lunch customers. The server should immediately help clean up the customer, then the server or a manager should offer to pay for the dry cleaning. Suggest that the customer send you the bill and you can take care of it for them. If a customer's food is wrong or prepared incorrectly, immediately get the food to the guest who has had to wait. To aid recovery in these situations, it might be a good idea to consider having a floater position. This person could work during the rush hours and basically wander through the restaurant ready to fix and forestall any problems.

- **Customer satisfaction survey.** Some people are shy about telling you they've had a bad experience in your restaurant. You can still get feedback from these more reticent customers by using customer satisfaction surveys. Have the server offer these with the check. They can be self-addressed and stamped for the customer to drop in the mail later, or they can fill them out and leave them at their table. You can share this feedback, good and bad, with your staff, later. Use the negative feedback to improve your restaurant. Use positive feedback to give specific employees accolades for their good work.

- **Be courteous.** Seems like common sense, but it's amazing how many servers don't treat guests with common courtesy. Make sure your servers say "thank you" and "you're welcome." The terms "ma'am" and "sir" are often appropriate as well.

- **Be knowledgeable.** One of the best resources your servers have for increasing their tips is to be knowledgeable about the menu. They should be able to tell a guest if the soup du jour is cream-based or if the shrimp is sautéed or grilled. Use language peppered with adjectives when describing menu items; you want to provide the customer with a mouth-watering mental image. For example, try saying, "Our special tonight is a rack of lamb, braised in a Merlot and rosemary broth and served with a savory wild mushroom bread pudding and fresh-roasted asparagus." Servers should also be well-informed about the establishment itself and be able to answer questions, such as operating hours, credit cards accepted and types of service available.

- **Acknowledge the customer quickly.** Customers need to be acknowledged within 60 seconds of being seated. Don't leave them waiting. Waiting will negatively affect a customer's mood, and a guest's mood is highly likely to affect the tip. If a server is swamped, train your host staff and bussers to help out. Even stopping for a second and saying "I'll be right with you," will make the customer comfortable in the knowledge that they will receive prompt, good service, within seconds.

- **Up-selling.** Up-selling will increase tips because you're increasing the total amount of the sale and most people tip on a percentage of the total. Have servers suggest appetizers, desserts and premium drinks. Don't let them strong-arm the guest, however. For instance, if a customer orders a gin and tonic, the server could say, "Do you prefer Tanguary, Beefeaters or our house gin?" This simple suggestion may influence a customer to order a call brand rather than a well brand.

- **Resolve problems.** Train your servers to resolve any problems – quickly. You also need to train the kitchen staff that problems need to be resolved immediately. If a customer gets the wrong order, or if their food is not prepared as they requested, tell your servers to apologize and offer to fix the problem. The server must also notify the kitchen that the replacement meal needs to be turned around quickly. If the server is unsure how to resolve a problem, you or a manager need to be available to come up with a solution. It's also a nice gesture to give the patron a break on the check. If someone ordered a medium-rare steak and was served a rare steak, make part of the apology a free round of drinks or dessert.

- **Show gratitude.** People are dealing with a lot in their lives and you have a chance to "make their day." Express gratitude in the tone of your voice when you thank them for their patronage. Making them feel appreciated will make them remember you – as they fill out the tip and the next time they're deciding where to eat!

Service – What Not to Do!

Just as there is a list of tried-and-tested procedures that make great service, there is also a list of things that will inevitably lead to poor service. Make sure your servers aren't engaging in any of the following practices:

- **All thumbs.** Clumsy servers not only look bad, but they can cause accidents. You can't enroll your servers in charm school, but you can give them tips on how to handle trays and plates. To avoid hiring someone that may not have the grace required, have applicants give a demonstration of their serving skills during the interview.

- **Unkempt appearance.** Be sure your servers' physical appearance makes a good impression on your guests. Servers' uniforms should be neat. All employees should be well-groomed and they should not smell offensive.

- **Attitude.** Don't let your servers get away with ignoring your guests. Even though some waitstaff do the job adequately, their attitude leaves a lot to be desired. Surly servers who seem to be in a hurry, or who fail to make eye contact, do nothing for your guests' appetites.

- **Don't be intrusive.** Customers want attention and service, not another person at the table. Train your waitstaff to be attentive, without being overbearing or intrusive. Servers should never get too personal with guests, nor should they engage in over-lengthy conversations.

Value-Added Service

How do you ensure that one-off customers become repeat patrons? The answer is simple: offer exceptional service. There are certain behaviors that servers should engage in to give good service, then there are behaviors that transform adequate service into value-added service. Many of the devices servers use to increase their tips are also devices that help you increase sales and profits. Encourage your servers to use some of these ploys:

- **Make recommendations.** If, for instance, a customer can't decide on an entrée or a wine, make sure your servers offer recommendations. For example, a server could say, "I tried the halibut special and it was divine!" Making suggestions can be very intuitive. Teach your servers to look for clues about what type of dining experience the patrons are after. Does it seem like a special occasion? If so, customers are more likely to order appetizers and desserts. Do they seem to be on a budget? Then suggest a mid- or lower-priced entrée. Remember, these are all suggestions; don't let the servers become pushy.

- **Remember guests' likes and dislikes.** Everyone likes to be remembered. If you have regular customers, encourage your servers to remember their specific food likes and dislikes. For example, if a couple comes in and always orders the same wine, have it ready for them next time before they ask for it. It's guaranteed to charm. It's likely that if they were going to order something different that evening, they will take "the usual" because they appreciate the server remembering their preference.

- **Be willing to customize.** If a customer asks for the steak without sauce, say "no problem!" If the customer wants to substitute rice for potatoes, do so without making a big fuss, checking with the kitchen or checking with the manager. Let your employees know ahead of time what they can offer without checking with someone. It will reflect on the server and you more positively if the server doesn't have to go and get permission for everything the customer wants!

- **Go beyond the call of duty.** Make the experience of dining at your restaurant unforgettable. Call a cab for the customer and offer a free beverage if they have a long wait. If it's raining, have someone escort the customer to the cab with an umbrella.

- **Suggest alternatives.** If the kitchen has sold out of a particular dish, or if dietary restrictions do not allow a patron to order a particular dish, servers should offer alternatives. If, for example there is a dairy product in the mashed potatoes and the guest is lactose intolerant, the server could suggest, "Our roasted potatoes are made with olive oil, perhaps you would like to substitute those?"

- **Single diners.** Single diners are often uncomfortable dining out. Unfortunately, servers can add to this discomfort by ignoring them. Make sure your servers pay attention to these single diners. Lone diners, however, often turn out to be business people who are using expense accounts, so the sales and tip potential are high. If the guest seems to want to be left alone, seat him or her in a secluded part of the dining room. If they seem eager to talk, spend a moment chatting. You can also offer a single diner reading material if you think that would make them more comfortable. Have reading materials available – and a staff that knows how to offer them politely.

- **Reinforce a guest's choice.** A couple decides to order a bottle of Merlot and are choosing between wine A and wine B. Compliment their decision.

Once a guest has placed an order, make them feel good about it. Tell them the strip flank steak looked excellent tonight or that the salmon just came in today. Don't tell them that the pork is a better choice than the steak! Encourage your guests' food choices. The simple act, on your part, of telling them that you've tasted what they're ordering and it's great, can take away any anxiety they have about making a bad choice.

- **Make personal recommendations.** Tell your guests what you like. This is not suggestive selling, because it's sincere and, therefore, won't alienate your guests. Your enthusiasm will be infectious, even if guests don't order what you recommend. It won't bother them that you're excited about what's on the menu.

- **Bring extra napkins.** If the guests order a meal that is particularly messy, such as barbecued ribs or lobster in butter sauce, bring them extra napkins before they ask. You should also provide extra napkins when customers dine with children.

- **Anticipate needs.** Bringing a customer something before they ask is an excellent way to win the customer over. Some servers seem to have a sixth sense about it. If you know a particular brand of scotch is very strong, for example, bring the guest a glass of water with the drink they requested. If you are serving red beans and rice, drop off the Tabasco sauce at the same time.

- **Coffee refills.** Make sure your servers provide coffee refills, but also be sure they ask before they pour. The guest might find it annoying to have the cup refilled without being asked. If a half-filled cup has been sitting for awhile, replace the cup with a fresh one rather than filling the lukewarm one.

- **Doggie bags.** Take an extra moment with the doggie bags. Rather than dropping a box off with the customer to fill, fill containers in the kitchen. Add a little something extra as well, perhaps a couple of pieces of bread or extra sauce. Also make sure you have appropriately sized and shaped containers for leftovers. When the customer arrives home and finds her flourless chocolate torte sideways in a soup container, it will not reflect well on the server, or the restaurant. For doggie bag sources, check with you local paper vending company. You also can find doggie bags online at McNairn Packaging, www.mcnairnpackaging.com/productinfo.asp?lstLine=B&lstCategory=6.

- **Keep an eye on your tables.** Even if a server is waiting on another table, he or she should keep their third eye on their other tables. If they see a guest looking around, stop over immediately and ask if there is anything you can get them.

- **Access for disabled.** Make sure that your restaurant is accessible for people with disabilities. Consider a ramp at the front door, if there are steps. Also have a table, or several tables, that have enough space to accommodate a wheel chair comfortably. If someone comes in for dinner who is blind, ask the guest if you can offer their seeing-eye dog some water or something to eat. For information about serving guests with disabilities, visit www.mtsu.edu/~adatech/Newsletter/whatetiquette2.htm or www.lascruces.org/Administration/ada/etiquette.htm.

- **Older guests.** Another way to give value-added service is to make special arrangements for older guests. Be sure servers are knowledgeable about the menu's nutritional content. Seat them in an area that provides good light for them to read the menu. Also, it's harder for the elderly to get in and out of their chairs, so have a few chairs with arms to make life easier for them. Let them know you did it just for them. Finally, ensure that servers respond to elderly customers with patience and respect. They will certainly appreciate it and tip accordingly!

- **Adding festivity.** Does someone at the table have a birthday? Give your servers ways to make the evening festive for the customers. Some restaurants have special desserts for birthdays and other occasions. Other establishments have the entire staff sing to the individual. Even a simple balloon at a table makes the evening seem a bit more festive.

- **Special requests.** Patrons will have special requests for various reasons. A customer may hate the taste of goat cheese and request a different type of cheese on the vegetarian sandwich. Some customers may also have special diets or food allergies to contend with. A restaurant that doesn't make a big fuss over "substitutions" can easily win the more restricted or finicky diner's heart!

- **Hooks for purses and coats.** If you don't have a coatroom, add hooks to booths for coats and purses, or provide coat trees in the lobby area.

- **Calculators with the check.** You may want to have a mini-calculator attached to your guest checkbooks. This will help customers figure out how to split bills and figure tips, without taxing their brains! If they've just enjoyed a relaxing dinner, your guests will appreciate the effort to keep them in that frame of mind!

- **Business customers.** Have your servers go the extra length for your business customers. Offer these guests quick service. You can also provide them with some additional services, such as copying, use of the phone and pads of paper and pens for making notes.

- **Umbrellas when it rains.** Is it possible that, given the weather patterns in your area, your guests could arrive without an umbrella, only to find it raining as they're leaving? Offer them umbrellas to help them get to their cars or offices. This could be a great incentive to have them come back at a later date to return the umbrella. Put your name and logo on the umbrella and maybe it's not the worst thing if they forget to bring it back!

- **Owner or manager on the floor.** People like to meet the person in charge. They appreciate that someone important is checking.

- **Fax directions to guests.** Have a great, clear map on hand and when guests ask for directions to your restaurant, offer to fax it to them. If they don't have a fax, make sure you can give them clear, explicit directions over the phone. Have the directions on your Web site, also. Don't have a Web site? Get one today! See www.gizwebs.com.

- **House camera.** If guests are celebrating but forgot a camera, have an instant camera on hand and snap a few shots for them to take home.

- **Don't ever think about the tip.** Focus your energy on taking care of your guests, making them happy, doing little things that exceed their expectations and generally making their meals as enjoyable as possible. That's how you will consistently get great tips.

- **Tell the cooks good news.** Just like you need to be sensitive to the mood of your guests, be sensitive to the mood of the kitchen crew. The cooks don't want to hear about things just when they're wrong. Pass along good news to them and they will probably make it easier for you to take great care of your guests.

- **Notice lefties.** It's a small thing, but if your guest has moved his water glass and/or silverware to the other side of his plate, serve his drinks from there. He'll appreciate it.

- **Make your movements invisible.** That means move with the speed of the room. Good service is invisible: food and drinks simply arrive without a thought on the customer's part. If the room is quiet, don't buzz around in it. If it's more upbeat, move a little quicker. You'll find fitting in seamlessly with the atmosphere will increase your guest's enjoyment – and it's a great way to stay focused.

- **Tell guests about specific events at your restaurant and invite them to return.** It provides an opportunity to build personal connections. For example, invite guests to return for your rib special on Tuesdays. It's far more effective than just saying, "Thanks, come again." While you're at it, invite them to sit at your station. You'll be more likely to remember their names and what they like.

Complimentary Items

People mind a wait a lot less when they've got a complimentary glass of wine or warm cider to keep them toasty, or the local paper or a magazine to read. They will appreciate you going the extra mile. It's something that distinguishes you from the competition and gives them something to talk about.

- **Free "goodies" while they wait.** Is there a long wait for a table in your restaurant on Saturday nights? Consider sending a server through the waiting area with a tray of appetizers for the people in line.

- **You may also want to offer complimentary items at the table**. If you have a bread basket, you could serve it with a bulb of roasted garlic and olive oil.

- **Consider offering complimentary coffee** with dessert. It's a low-cost way to win customers.

- **"Tasters."** A good come-on is to give patrons sips of wine or small tasters of your specialty dishes – but only enough to whet the appetite!

- **Free local calls – with a portable phone.** This can be a huge convenience for guests, allowing them to change travel plans, contact friends and handle nagging details – at virtually no cost to you.

Let customers know that you offer this service; it will help set you apart from the competition.

- **Give people something for nothing.** Got some new menu items coming up next week? Why not give away free samples today! There's nothing customers like more than something for nothing, and it's another great way to distinguish you from the competition.

- **Free postcards and postage.** Do a lot of tourist business? If your guests are waiting – or even if they aren't – why not give them stamped postcards (depicting your restaurant, of course) for sending their "Wish you were here" messages? It's a very low price to pay for giving your guests something they'll appreciate and enabling them to send your advertising all over the world.

Take Care of the Kids

More and more restaurant owners are realizing the importance of kid appeal. Children have a large influence on where the family dines. To gain the customer loyalty of children and their families, you must create a kid-friendly environment. Your servers play a big role in making an establishment kid-friendly, but so do you. Give your servers tools they can use to attain this goal. Here are some suggestions:

- **Provide kids with menus to color.** Have plenty of crayons or games at the ready, to keep the kids occupied until the food is served. Two companies where you can find crayons, kid place mats and table toys are:
  - Binney & Smith, Inc., www.binney-smith.com

- Sherman Specialty Co., Inc., www.shermanspecialty.com

- **Speedy service.** Make sure your staff serves children's drinks and something to munch on as quickly as possible if it looks like the order may take a little while. Granted, your servers aren't babysitters, but anything they can do to help the parents have a relaxing meal and to entertain the kids will be welcomed by your guests with children. Paying attention to kids also helps your other customers, since an occupied child is less likely to be a screaming child!

  - **Train your servers to talk to the kids** as well as to the parents.

  - **Make sure you have plenty of high chairs and booster seats.** If possible, have these seats ready, before the party is seated.

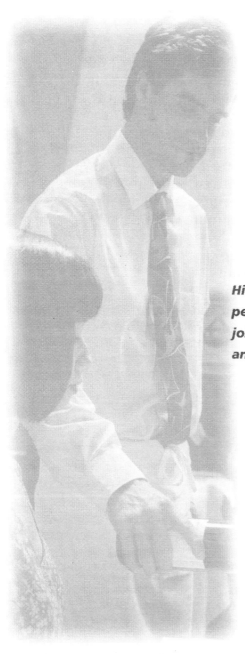

Hire the right person for the job to save time and money.

CHAPTER THREE

HIRING AND TERMINATING

Hiring – Essential Information

The first step in developing a staff that will maximize profits is to hire the right people from the start. By hiring the right persons for the job, you save money and time on searching for, hiring and training replacements. You also have less turnover and fewer morale problems to worry about. Here are some essential tips to help you make a success of the hiring process:

- **Federal regulations.** There are a lot of federal regulations concerning hiring employees, so make sure you know the rules before you start. A great resource for federal laws is the U.S. Department of Labor's Employment Law Handbook. To access this information, see www.dol.gov/asp/programs/handbook/main2.htm.

- **The U.S. Department of Labor's Elaws,** www.dol.gov/elaws, provides business owners with interactive tools that give information about federal employment laws.

- **Uniform Guidelines on Selection Procedures** is another useful guide for making hiring decisions. This can be viewed at www.uniformguidelines.com/uniformguidelines.html#3.

- **Human resource information.** The Council on

Education in Management's Web site, www.counciloned.com, is a good human resources source for information and training.

The Application

Always have job candidates fill out an application form. The application form gives you information on the person's skills and experience. The following tips will help you streamline your application process:

- **Application file.** You should keep applications on file for a year. It is a good source to use to look for potential employees the next time you have an opening. Rather than advertising, look at your application file first. Was there anyone who stood out that you didn't have an opening for before?

- **References.** Make sure your application form has a spot for the candidate to list references. Use this information! Many future problems can be avoided if you call two or three references. Ask the referee what job the candidate performed, what time period they worked for the referee, if the candidate got along with supervisors and co-workers, if the referee would ever consider hiring them again.

- **Tests.** You may want to consider including job skills tests in your application process. Perhaps you could give the candidate a short math test or ask him or her to demonstrate how they would wait on a customer.

Job Descriptions

Many restaurants have functioned for years without written job descriptions. But, having job descriptions not only makes your life easier; it can also help protect you in the event of wrongful termination suits! A job description should include:

- **Components of a job description:**
  - The job title

  - Name of supervisor

  - A summary of the job

  - Tasks (an outline of the job's duties)

  - Experience and skills required, (this includes number of years of previous experience, math skills, educational level, etc.)

  - Working conditions (e.g., if the job involves heavy lifting, air-conditioned facility, long hours on feet, etc.)

- **Reasons for having job descriptions.** There are many reasons, including they help you select qualified employees in the first place. Job descriptions also help new hires know what you expect from the position. They can also be used as training checklists and, as previously stated, they are important documents in wrongful termination and discrimination lawsuits. Finally, job descriptions are good measuring sticks for performance review evaluations.

- **The following page has an example of a server's job description:**

JOB DESCRIPTION

Job Title: Server

Supervisor: Assistant Manager

Summary: The server's main job function is to take care of serving guests in a timely manner. The essential functions of this position include:

Job Duties:

- Take food and drinks orders;
- Deliver orders to the guest in a timely fashion;
- Serve food;
- Refill beverages;
- Process customers' payments;
- Clear tables; and
- Set up tables at beginning of shift. This includes refilling salt and pepper shakers and setting silverware and linen.
- Side duties include preparing bread baskets, setting up salad bar and assisting bartender; and
- Restocking service area.

Required Skills and Qualifications:

- Outgoing, pleasant personality;
- Desire to please guests/customers;
- Math skills;
- Previous restaurant experience;
- Ability to lift 30 pounds and stand for 8 hours; and
- Ability to work in a team environment.

Working conditions: The person in this position will work in an air-conditioned restaurant facility. The job requires long hours on feet, lifting, carrying, walking and bending.

- **Resources for writing job descriptions.** Check out the job description and employee handbook software at Atlantic Publishing, www.atlantic-pub.com, 800-541-1336. You can also get information on writing job descriptions and other staff management issues by attending one of the organization's Restaurant Staff Management workshops. The Restaurant Workshop at www.restaurantworkshop.com also has information regarding writing job descriptions.

Interviewing

The application will give you some information about a potential employee, but the job interview will give you more. When interviewing, don't use a script; have a conversation. Focus on what animates the candidate. Ask open-ended questions and look for thoughtful responses. Also have other employees participate in the interview process so that you can compare impressions. Look for new hires who will be amenable to cross-training and new opportunities. Ask how they feel about taking on new responsibilities and what other positions they would like to learn. Here are some guidelines that will help you through the interviewing process:

- **What you should bring to the interview.** Be systematic. Before you go into an interview, prepare a list of questions. Also, be sure to read the application before you sit down for the interview. Have the job description, expected work hours, pay information and general restaurant policies in front of you. Discuss these details with the candidate. Inform the applicant of the time frame in which he or she will be notified about the position. Ask if the applicant has any questions before you finish the interview.

- **Where to interview.** Conduct interviews in a quiet place, such as a back table during a slow period. Most restaurant owners and managers like to hold interviews and accept applications in the mid- to late-afternoon hours between lunch and dinner rushes. Be sure to eliminate distractions. Ask your staff not to interrupt you and leave your cell phone and pager on your desk.

- **Develop a rapport.** Job interviews are stressful. Take a few moments at the beginning of interviews to chat and put the applicant at ease. This will let the person relax and the interview will be more successful.

- **First impressions.** The interview is where you get your first impression of your potential employee. Notice what they are wearing. Remember, this is the first impression your customers will get as well. You can also get a feeling for their punctuality. Did they arrive on time? Better yet, did they arrive 5 minutes early? Do they seem organized? Do they have all the information they need to fill out the application?

- **What to look for in a person you are hiring as a server.** Look for a passion for service. Often, this is more important than a lot of past experience. People with non-traditional backgrounds are often more flexible. Also, remember that people skills are more important than technical skills. You can easily teach the technical skills. Does the candidate look you in the eye? Does he or she smile? Do they seem warm and friendly or aloof? What does their body language tell you? Someone who sits back with their arms folded sends a negative signal. Someone sitting forward, however, signals interest and eagerness. Look for servers with outgoing personalities who will be good salespeople.

- **Questions you cannot ask in an interview.** While no particular question is expressly prohibited under federal law, the EEOC frowns upon questions that directly or indirectly ask about race, religion, sex, national origin or age. It is inappropriate, for example, to ask women about their family obligations or if they plan to become pregnant. If you are unsure whether a question is appropriate, play it safe and don't ask. Here are a few examples of appropriate and inappropriate questions to ask in an interview:

  - **Inappropriate** (possibly illegal): *How old are you?*
    Appropriate: *Are you over 18?* (Check your state liquor laws and be sure to ask if they are old enough to serve alcohol.)

  - **Inappropriate:** *Do you have any physical defects?*
    Appropriate: *Do you have a disability that would negatively affect your job performance?*

  - **Inappropriate:** *What is your religion?*
    Appropriate: Don't ask, but you may want to provide them with the work schedule so they can tell you if it interferes with religious services.

  - **Inappropriate:** *Are you married?*
    Appropriate: Don't ask. You can ask for contact information for a person in case of an emergency, however.

- **Inappropriate:** *Have you ever been arrested?*
  Appropriate: *Have you ever been convicted of a criminal offense?*

- **Inappropriate:** *How much do you weigh?*
  Appropriate: Don't ask.

- **Further information.** For more information about legal and appropriate interview strategies, visit www.doi.gov/hrm/pmanager/st13c3.html and www.doi.gov/hrm/pmanager/st13c.html. The National Restaurant Association also offers a publication entitled The Legal Problem Solver for Restaurant Operators. You can order the publication online at www.restaurant.org.

- **Questions you'll want to ask.** Start out by reviewing the applicant's work history. You should also ask if anything would interfere with the person getting to work on time. You should ask specifics about experience. Has the candidate ever served wine? How many tables have they waited on at one time? Have they made salads before? You may also want to give the candidate hypothetical questions to answer to see how they would react in particular situations. For example, ask the candidate, "If a customer sent back a freshly opened bottle of wine, what would you do?" or "It's a Saturday night, one of the other servers has called in sick and the salad person has just walked out. How would you react?" These types of questions can tell you about job knowledge and how well a person works under stress.

- **Open-ended questions.** Some of the questions will only require a yes or no answer. For example, "Have you worked as a server before?" You should also ask open-ended questions to give the applicant an opportunity to talk. Remember, a job applicant should do about 80 percent of all the talking. For instance, you could ask an applicant to describe what they liked best about their previous job.

- **Take notes.** Make sure to take notes during the interview. This will make it easier to compare potential candidates when you make your hiring decision.

- **A panel interview. In restaurants, interviews are typically conducted by managers.** You may want to think about including others in the interview process. If you're hiring a new server, for instance, you may want the serving captain to interview with you. This person may think to ask important questions you wouldn't. Do not include too many people, however, or you're likely to make the candidate a bundle of nerves!

- **Rehiring.** Consider rehiring talented former employees. By rehiring someone, you will save time and money on retraining. Do not, however, just throw the person back on the front lines. Give the rehire the same information as new hires and give them the appropriate amount of training.

- **Interview red flags.** Watch out for individuals that show too much interest in hours, benefits, wages and titles during the interview process. This interest can signal a person that isn't too interested in work. Also, look for long lapses of time in the work history section of the application. Ask the person what they did during this time. They may simply have taken time out to raise children or it could signal a trouble spot.

- **Recruiting for teamwork.** When hiring, you want to find people who are going to pitch in and help. Basically, you want people who can function well as part of a team. When recruiting, avoid superstars and seek both technical skills and evidence of being good with people. You may want to ask about teams they have been on (sports or other). Also ask how they may have handled conflict with fellow workers in the past.

- **The four types of "team player personality styles."** In general, there are four personality types that function well in a team environment. The best teams have a balance of all four and members. Understand the different types and roles. Keep your eyes open for these types of individuals:
  - The contributor. Technically adept, task-oriented, born trainer. Excellent leader in kitchen or detail-oriented bus staff.

  - The collaborator. Goal-oriented, quick to help out. Excellent in front-of-the-house staff.

  - The communicator. Process-oriented, great floor manager, server, greeter – good trainer, attentive listening skills for problem solving.

  - The challenger. Candor and openness helps a team explore better ways of doing things. Highly principled, willing to disagree, blow whistle.

Employee Orientations

Every new employee should receive an orientation to your business and their job. All too often restaurant owners throw their employees to the wolves, the first shift, because they are short-staffed and shortsighted. Orientation includes:

- **Tour.** One of the first things you should do is give the new employee a tour of the facility. Make sure to point out where they can put their belongings and where they can take breaks, as well as areas for employee notices.

- **Introductions.** It's also important to introduce the new person to their fellow workers. When making the introductions, point out people the new employee can turn to for guidance. Let them know who the team leader of the shift is and who has been around for awhile and will be able to answer questions.

- **Hiring paperwork.** This is a good time to have the employee fill out hiring papers. These papers should include the I-9 form, tax paperwork and a personnel data sheet for whom to contact, in case of emergency. It's also a good idea to check with your local government agencies about additional paperwork they may require.

- **Orientation materials.** Here is a list of things you may want to include in the orientation packet:
  - Scheduling procedures
  - Uniform requirements
  - Employee benefits
  - Employee meal policy
  - Tip reporting procedure
  - Policy on employee eating or drinking, as customer while off shift
  - Pay periods and clocking in and out procedures
  - Job description

- Safety and emergency plans
- Copy of the menu and wine list
- Copy of an employee call list

- **Online resources.** A good online resource for information on how to develop an orientation program is "Deliver the Promise" at www.deliver-thepromise.com. This site also offers information on strategies to retain employees, as well as mentoring and coaching. They also offer an online employee orientation. Also visit HP Invent at www.hp.com/education/courses/orient_service.html for information on their employee orientation service.

Recruiting Sources

So where do you find good employees? Running an advertisement in the local paper is always the first thing that comes to mind, but this may not be your best resource for employees. Consider the following alternatives as well:

- **Promoting from within.** Promoting from within is an excellent source. Hosts and bus people are often anxious to be promoted to serving staff because of the increase in income and prestige. Not only does this method motivate your current workers, but it saves you money on training because these people already know a great deal about the establishment and position. It's much easier and cheaper to find bussers and hosts/hostesses from the outside and train them than to recruit and train a new server.

- **Employee referrals.** Ask your employees if they

have friends or relatives who are looking for work. Often, an employee won't recommend a friend unless they are sure this friend is not going to embarrass them by doing a poor job, so you are likely to get good new employees this way! Offer an incentive to employees for helping you recruit. You could offer an employee a $25 bonus for each referral; if the person works out and stays on for a year, give both the employee and new hire a cash bonus at the end of that year.

- **Open house.** Hold an open house to find new employees. This strategy is particularly effective if you're looking to fill several positions at once. These take more work than a regular interview, but it may be worth it. Get your managers or other employees to help. Make sure to advertise the open house.

- **Off-site recruiting.** Restaurant trade shows are excellent places to recruit! Consider using other events for recruitment purposes, such as wine tastings, food festivals and career fairs.

- **Customers.** Got a regular customer looking for employment? What a great source! You know they already like your restaurant so they'll probably make a good salesperson too!

- **Industry organizations and Web sites.** Many industry Web sites have pages for posting jobs and resumés. Check out a few of the following sites:
  - National Restaurant Association, www.restaurant.org

  - Restaurantbeast.com, www.restaurantbeast.com

  - Nation's Restaurant News, www.nrn.com

- **Area colleges.** Many college students are looking for a source of income and a schedule that can work around their classes. Many of these colleges also offer culinary arts or restaurant management programs. Check out Texas State Community College at www.waco.tstc.edu or Phoenix College at www.pc.maricopa.edu/index.html.

- **Culinary schools.** Check out local and national culinary schools. They usually have a spot on their Web sites for people to post resumés. Some examples include: CIA, www.ciachef.edu; Sullivan's University in Louisville, Kentucky, www.sullivan.edu/programs/program2.htm; and New England Culinary Institute, www.neculinary.com. The National Restaurant Association's Web sites has a listing of culinary/hospitality schools across the country. For more information, log on to www.restaurant.org/careers/schools.cfm.

CHAPTER FOUR

RETAINING YOUR SERVICE STAFF

Turnover

The restaurant industry is notorious for being unable to retain good employees. High employee turnover sends a bad message to both employees and customers. Customers won't receive the best service you can offer because you're constantly training new people – and employees' morale drops. High turnover rates indicate a problem that should be investigated. But, before you try to fix the problem, determine the cause. Here are some excellent strategies for retaining your employees.

- **Recruiting.** Recruit the right people to work in your restaurant. Determine the type of worker you need before deciding what recruiting sources to use. If you own a fine-dining establishment and you need highly skilled servers, look on industry Web sites, use employment services, employee referrals and hospitality school students. You'll get a higher-skilled server from these sources than someone walking in off the street or answering a newspaper ad.

- **Interviewing.** Explain to the interviewees exactly what the job entails. Give them as much information as you can about the job and find out as much as you can about them. Be sure to check references!

- **Training.** Give your employees the tools they need to do a good job. Don't just hire your staff then let them go about their business. Train and retrain your staff. Communicate to them what you need them to do and how you want them to do it.

- **Communication.** Keep the lines of communication open with your servers. Poor communication leads to employee frustration and dissatisfaction, poorer service and higher turnover. Training is a form of communication, but there are many other·possibilities. Post a bulletin board for important news or new information. For example, if you have a new menu item, put up a description and a picture of what the dish should look like. Communicate on a daily basis. An open-door policy for employees' suggestions and/or problems goes a long way in keeping the communication lines open.

- **Exit interviews.** When someone does leave, make sure to hold an exit interview. Exit interviews can tell you why the person is leaving and they may be helpful for finding ways to improve your establishment. You can also find out why people like to work for you! Exit interviews are set up the same way as hiring interviews. Be sure to hold the exit interview in a private, quiet place. Questions to ask during an exit interview include:
    - What did you like and dislike about working here?

    - What type of skills/qualities should your replacement have?

    - What does your new employer offer that we don't?

Updating Your Compensation System

These days many businesses are seeing changes in compensation systems. Take a look at the following issues:

- **Tip policy changes.** The reason some restaurants are changing how they view compensation is because management recognizes the importance of teamwork. If you're going to ask all your staff to team up serving the customer, then why should only one server reap the benefit? Such a result undermines the teamwork concept. Rather than a server keeping all of his or her tips for the night, the staff is better off pooling and dispersing the tips for the shift.

- **Explain the changes to your staff.** Begin by explaining the new compensation idea and by tracking what would be the case if you took all the tips and pooled them. Let your servers discover what the result would have been over a period of time. This should show servers that they can make as much, if not more, money this way.

- **Show them the difference.** Have them work a week of not helping each other, followed by a week of helping while everyone keeps track of tips and results are recorded. Most likely the result will convince your employees of the benefits of a new compensation system and they will ask for it!

- **Other ways to update your compensation system.** Keep current with wage survey information and make sure you are competitive. A good resource for information on restaurant wages is the U.S. Department of Labor's Bureau of

Statistics' Web site at www.bls.gov/oes/2000/
oes_35fo.htm. Also check out your direct
competition to see how they are compensating
employees. Do they offer sick time or health
benefits? To retain your best servers, you really
need to consider staying competitive in the salary
and benefits area.

Benefits

The restaurant industry has a poor reputation for
rewarding its employees through high wages and
benefits. This reputation is changing, however. Many
restaurants are beginning to offer their employees the
following work incentives:

- **Required benefits.** Employers are legally required
  to provide their employees with Social Security
  benefits, unemployment insurance and workers'
  compensation insurance. To find out more about
  these benefits, visit the U.S. Department of Labor
  at www.dol.gov. You should advertise these as
  benefits to your employees. When you're hiring,
  provide the employee with a list of benefits and
  include the benefits listed above.

- **Discretionary benefits.** These benefits include
  health and dental benefits, vacation time, sick
  time, paid holidays, life insurance, disability
  insurance and retirement plans. While these
  benefits can be expensive, they can also help you
  attract and retain great employees. Look at your
  profit and loss statements and see if you can work
  some of these benefits into your expenses.

- **Health plan information.** For more information

on health and dental benefits, contact a plan administrator. Some of the larger health insurance companies include Anthem, www.anthem.com; Aetna, www.aetna.com; and Cigna, www.cigna.com.

- **Burnout insurance.** Offering vacation and sick time is a good way to keep your staff from burning out. Develop a way of tracking this time and a policy for how to request time off.

- **Creative retirement plans.** Most small restaurants can't afford retirement plans, but perhaps you can help employees with retirement in other ways. Consider paying for employees to attend retirement-planning seminars. You can also find a financial planning firm to work with to set up IRAs for your employees and let them contribute to their IRAs through payroll deduction.

Incentives

Incentives are another important way to show your employees that they're doing a good job. Incentives also help to retain and motivate your staff. Reward outstanding performance. You may wish to consider some of the following popular incentives:

- **Bonuses.** Consider awarding bonuses for the exemplary performance of an individual or an entire team. These don't always have to be large. A $25 bonus goes a long way in telling an employee "thank you for the hard work."

- **Salary increases.** Salary increases are an excellent way to reward outstanding performance. Be sure to provide annual performance evaluations and link salary increases to these evaluations. Also watch that sales incentives don't cancel out attention to other details of team goals.

- **Promotions.** Have a promote-from-within policy and use it. This policy should include promoting from one position to another, such as busser to server. It should also include more subtle ways of adding job responsibilities and pay. Create rotating team leaders within your staff. For example, use your five best servers to train new hires. When they are training, give them a wage increase. This is particularly important if training someone new means they won't be making tips that shift!

Firing

Firing is a fact of life, in all industries. Given the number of people you employ, during the course of your restaurant career, it is almost guaranteed that you will someday have to fire someone. Here are some issues to keep in mind when the occasion does arise:

- **Have an employment-at-will statement in your handbook.** Include an employment-at-will statement in your employee handbook that the employee signs. This statement basically says that the employer or employee can terminate employment at any time. Don't say that you can only terminate an employee for just cause; this can be interpreted as a guarantee of employment in court and this will work against you in legal situations.

- **Use restaurant policies.** Create and use job descriptions. If you use job descriptions, you can show that employees know what's expected of them in order to continue in employment. Also make sure you perform staff evaluations on a regular basis.

- **Have a disciplinary process in place.** Make sure employees know about it. You should provide this information to all new hires during their orientation. What type of policy you have is up to you, but in general, companies use a progressive disciplinary policy. Basically, this method uses progressive corrective measures; managers who use it hope the employee will correct their own inappropriate behavior. This procedure usually includes four steps: oral warning or counseling, written warning, suspension and, finally, termination.

- **Keep a paper trail.** In this day and age of litigation, you must keep records if you need to fire someone. Use your disciplinary procedures as a guide for your actions, then be sure to include any paperwork in the employee's personnel file.

- **Make firing a last resort.** You should fire an employee only after you have tried everything else. Talk to the employee first and explain the problem, suggesting ways to improve. If things don't get any better, put the matter in writing to the employee and place the notice in his or her personnel file. Then, discipline his or her next occurrence of inappropriate behavior. Finally, if nothing else works, fire the employee.

- **Be professional.** Firing someone can be unnerving for the person doing the firing and emotionally traumatic for the person being fired. Do it in the privacy of your office so you don't embarrass the person needlessly. In addition, don't make it personal; don't argue about old disputes and talk about personality traits. Let the person know why you are letting them go and do it in a calm, professional manner.

- **Timing.** If it's possible, don't fire someone on his or her birthday, at Christmas or at any other time that is a special occasion.

- **Set a date.** Be sure to set an exact date that the employee's employment is terminated. Also discuss any benefits or monetary issues, such as COBRA insurance, the return of uniforms, accrued vacation time and last paycheck disbursement.

- **Debrief the staff.** After you let someone go, call the rest of the staff together to explain honestly why it was necessary. This will keep everyone in the loop and prevent gossip and help head off any morale problems.

CHAPTER FIVE

TRAINING YOUR SERVICE STAFF

When to Train

Training is probably the most important step in staff development. While a training program is time consuming, it can lead to upgrading of customer orders and increased numbers of customers. Increased customer satisfaction means increased profits. Training, however, takes time, planning and dedication. So, when are the best times for training?

- **New hires.** All new hires always require training. Even if the person has worked as a server for 20 years, that person has not worked for you as a server. Make sure you train all new hires to give the quality of service you expect at your establishment.

- **Customer satisfaction surveys.** Comments on customer surveys may indicate it is time for retraining. If you consistently see comment cards that say "Our server didn't know anything about the wine list," it's time for a wine-training session.

- **Turnover.** Have you suffered from high turnover recently? It may be good to get the whole staff together for training, just to be sure everyone is "on the same page."

- **Regular training.** You should also hold regular

retraining sessions for all staff. Once a week is overkill, but bimonthly or quarterly is an excellent idea. Pick specific topics for each session, rather than trying to cover everything.

- **Preshift.** Many fine-dining establishments, such as Charlie Trotter's restaurants, hold a brief pre-shift training meeting. This session should take no longer than 15 minutes. It should contain information on the specials and any current problems or new issues.

What Makes a Successful Trainer?

More than likely you or one of your managers will do the majority of the training in your establishment. Here are a few instructor traits to keep in mind when preparing for a training session:

- **Is respected.** It's much easier to get someone to follow if they respect the leader. Staff will not respect what you tell them unless they know you do the same work. If you're training servers, for instance, make sure your servers see you on the floor taking orders and bussing tables – the right way. They will be more inclined to follow your example and respect the information you pass on to them.

- **Uses past mistakes to illustrate.** Give your serving staff true examples and let them learn from others! If you use examples from your own establishment, be careful not to embarrass anyone.

- **Illustrates with real life examples.** If your servers

get a glazed look in their eyes every time you talk about food safety, bring in some examples. You can get online and find dozens of food-borne illness incidents. Bring those in to share with servers. Better yet, have the servers do the research and tell them to bring the examples to the next meeting. By showing them that this really does happen, you make the knowledge more meaningful.

- **Gives breaks.** Don't try to run a meeting past 50-60 minutes without a break. People's minds start to wander; their bodies need a break as well. You may want to have refreshments of some sort for the break periods.

- **Divides information into manageable portions.** Don't try to throw the entire training manual at your staff in one session, as they'll only retain a portion of what you want them to know. If you have a lot of material to cover, do it in several meetings. Also be sure to organize your material for each meeting.

- **Demonstrates and repeats material.** By demonstrating and repeating information, you will help your staff retain it.

- **Learning personalities.** When training, keep in mind that there are many styles of learning. Some people learn better through practical application, others are visual learners and some people learn by listening. Aim for a balance of methods during a single training session. You could talk for part of the session and then show a video. You could also use role-playing exercises or games.

- **Training resource.** The American Management Association offers a "Training the Trainer" course. You can find information about the seminar at www.amanet.org/seminars/cmd2/8507.htm.

New Hires

Before you can implement a training process in your establishment, you need to determine your goals and the behavior and attitude you desire and expect from your new staff. Keep in mind that it takes approximately 21 days of different behavior to change a habit. Here are some practical tips for training new hires:

- **Begin training on the first day of a server's employment.** This will help ease first-day nervousness. One of the first things you should do is give them a tour and introduce them to everyone.

- **Team spirit from the outset.** If several employees begin on the same day, even though for different jobs, let them begin orientation together. Build camaraderie and let them learn about how their job fits in with other jobs.

- **Communicating with new hires.** Make sure new employees know it's all right to ask questions. Give reasons for procedures in layperson's terms; there will be enough time to teach them your restaurant's specific shorthand phrases after they have been oriented.

- **Build confidence.** Teach some things they can do the first day to build confidence, such as helping set out waters or filling bread baskets. When you do need to correct behavior, show them a better way rather than criticizing their actions. If your new hire has a tray of water glasses and is filling each one with the ice scoop, rather than yelling "That's the slow way!" suggest using a plastic pitcher to take the ice from the machine and fill the glasses from there.

- **Get other employees involved in training.** Give a bonus/award to a trainer if the new hire stays at least 30 or 60 days. This will make servers more willing to help train and it will influence them to teach appropriate behavior rather than sloppy habits. New hires should also spend time in the kitchen, to understand the flow, how food is prepared, how food should taste and to get a feel for the timing.

- **Give new hires an overview of your restaurant.** Consider starting them as dishwashers or bussers and let them work up through each function, including both front-of-the-house and the kitchen. This will allow the new hire to see how all jobs interact and how each person affects the other. Meanwhile, do cross-training for everyone else. Cross-training also means that, at a push, anyone can fill in for anyone else. It also allows you to promote experienced employees from within. This can save you a great deal in training and hiring costs. Finally, your customers will benefit from it because they will receive improved and seamless service.

Training Methods

You should hold training sessions periodically throughout the year to refresh servers' memories.

This is especially important if you have a new menu or there are other major changes taking place in your restaurant. Keep your regular training sessions short; try not to go over 90 minutes and only try to cover 3 or 4 topics. Minimize distractions. Do not, for example, try to hold a session during a regular shift. Appeal to all senses; use flip charts with colored markers, videos, workbooks and tokens for rewards. Include role-playing to reinforce retention of lessons learned. Pick the training method that is best suited to the topic. Also, don't use just one method throughout the training session. Try a combination of the following methods:

- **Role playing.** This is a good way to let servers practice their skills. Have scenarios made up in advance and written on cards. Also prepare some possible customer dialogue in advance; this will help keep the training session moving. During the session, jot down a few specific functional behaviors, such as "learning and remembering a guest's name," "offering a choice," "up-selling," "explaining that there is no more lobster," etc. Then, call upon participants to act out the roles of server and customer, making sure everyone gets a turn. Critique each performance by first asking the others for comments, "What was good, what could have been better?" Add your own comments only if specific points haven't been raised. Write down on the flip chart any missed opportunities. Near the end of session time, review the main points covered and ask, "What will you do differently now as a result of today's exercises?" You don't have to relegate role playing to quarterly or yearly meetings, schedule mini-role-playing opportunities into as many pre-shift or other meetings as possible.

- **Shadowing.** There are two ways to shadow: the

new hire shadows an experienced worker or an experienced worker shadows the new hire. In general, it is good to have a new employee simply follow someone else around on their shift for the first couple of days. Once it seems obvious that the new hire is catching on, the roles can reverse. New servers are shadowed by an experienced one, for whatever length of time it takes – it might be 2-12 months.

- **Cross-training.** Cross-training is a great training technique to use with your existing staff. This type of training will allow people to experience the problems of·employees in other positions. As a result, your establishment will become more efficient and your guests will receive better service. Develop and post a cross-training schedule. Let your servers spend a couple of shifts with the cooks and a couple with the bussers and the host/hostess. This type of training is extremely cost-effective.

- **Classroom.** Some types of training may require classroom time. It's a good idea to train your staff about food safety and first aid with an expert; you can find classes at many area colleges and vocational schools. There also are many companies that specialize in one-day seminars with topics such as customer service or dealing with difficult people.

- **Also try Seminar Information Service, Inc.'s** Web site at www.seminarinformation.com/ index.cfm?refer=GGL. While this training is not specialized for the restaurant industry, it can give your staff some very useful, basic information.

- **Videos.** There are many training subjects that can be found on video. See www.atlantic-pub.com for a complete resource of food service training tapes. These subjects range from sexual harassment to food safety to cooking. Videos are a good way to enhance your regular training session. Rather than talking the entire time, use some of the meeting time for a video so your staff has some variety in the training session.

- **Training material for the hospitality industry.** All sorts of training material for the hospitality industry may be found at Atlantic Publishing Company, www.atlantic-pub.com, 800-541-1336.

- **Computer training (CD or online).** The restaurant industry, like so many other industries can offer many courses and training subjects to their employees, either online or on a CD. The benefits of this type of training include being able to work at your own pace and being cost-effective. Here are some resources for this type of training:
  - Campus 2 Go's Web site offers coursework in food safety and restaurant management; www.Campus2Go.com

  - The American Hotel and Motel Association's Educational Institute offers distance learning courses in food safety, food and beverage service and management; www.ei-ahla.org

  - This site offers courses in food safety, food and beverage service and management among many others; www.restaurantworkshop.com

  - ServSafe® Manager Certification Training; www.atlantic-pub.com

- **Games.** A fun way to train your servers is to use games. For menu training, you can play a version of charades. Write several menu items down on pieces of paper and divide the serving staff into two teams. One person on each team chooses a menu item; the rest of the team has to guess. Let your servers do the talking. If the menu item is shrimp cocktail, for instance, they could say, "It's served with a tomato-based sauce." Use a timer for the game and award a prize to the team who guesses in the least amount of time.

- **Professional trainers.** You can hire professional trainers to come and work with your staff. The Restaurant Doctor provides half-day staff training seminars. To find out more, log on to www.restaurantdoctor.com. The Council of Hotel and Restaurant Trainers (CHART) is also a good source. CHART is a professional association of hospitality training professionals. The organization helps food service training professionals improve their service and their business by developing their staff. For more information, visit their Web site at www.chart.org. The Society for Food Service Management is another online resource for development at www.sfm-online.org.

Training Manual

Provide all your employees with a written manual. Include general restaurant information as well as specifics about the job. New employees should be given a manual within their first few days of employment and should sign a statement confirming that they've read and understood the contents. Keep this statement in the employee's personnel file. Also keep a copy of training manuals on hand for employees to refer to during work hours. The servers' manual should include the following topics:

- Restaurant policies
- Safety plan
- Job description
- Scheduling procedures
- Dress code/uniform requirements
- Employee benefits and pay information
- Employee meal policy
- Tip reporting procedures
- Clocking in and out procedures
- Guest check accountability
- Setup procedures
- Menu and description of each menu item and specialty drinks and wine list
- Frequently asked customer questions and answers
- Information on accommodating special diets
- How to approach the customer
- How to take the order
- Standard guest check abbreviations
- Table and station numbers
- How to write a guest check
- How to up-sell and make suggestions
- How to place the order with the kitchen
- How to place bar orders
- Service standards
- Procedures for checking back with customers
- Correct bussing procedures
- Closing and check-out procedures
- Station setup for next shift
- Turning over customers to another server
- How to stock for next shift
- Cleaning responsibilities

Effective Staff Meetings

Most staff meetings are far from invigorating. In fact, they usually result in a drop in energy and a staff that feels they are on management's bad side. So, how are you going to impart new information and team spirit to your staff and how are you going to get them excited about delighting your customers? You need a great, truly effective staff meeting. Consider the following important issues:

- **Two-way dialog.** An effective staff meeting is not just a gathering of bodies with one person giving out information; it's primarily a meeting that generates positive feeling throughout the entire group. An effective staff meeting has three main goals:
  - Generating positive group feeling
  - Starting a dialogue
  - Training

- **Positive group feeling.** This will help your staff discover what it has in common and think in terms of working together, as opposed to functioning as individuals. Share good news in order to build good feeling. Staff meetings are not a good time to address individual or group shortcomings. Find the positive – even if you need to hunt for it – and talk about it. This is one of the best ways to build a supportive feeling and get people talking.

- **Dialogue.** A good dialogue is a comfortable back-and-forth of ideas that gets people connected and leaves your staff feeling that they're a truly creative part of your restaurant. You learn from the staff – and they learn from you. Allowing this flow of ideas reduces or eliminates the "us vs. them" mentality. If everybody feels part of the same team, service improves and productivity and profits go up.

- **Training.** Good staff meetings are places to pass on ideas for better performance and to allow servers to pick up tips and learn from each other. Your staff members are intelligent and they instinctively know what works. Encouraging them to share thoughts about work will turn staff meetings into a forum for discussing ideas. This atmosphere will increase their learning curve dramatically.

- **Camaraderie.** Becoming good at running staff meetings will translate into a feeling of camaraderie among your staff. They won't just be giving you the true insights into how your business is being run; they'll be caring about how to improve it, because they know their suggestions count. You will be more effective, because your staff will take weight off your shoulders, helping your restaurant run better and making your job a lot more pleasant.

Pre-Shift Meetings

Ideally, you should hold a staff meeting before every shift, every day. If you cancel staff meetings frequently, it sends the message that they're not important and that the staff's opinions are equally unimportant. Use the meeting as an opportunity to set the day's responsibilities for each member and to encourage participation by all. Have executives attend meetings for added impact. An effective pre-shift meeting should last no longer than 15 minutes. If it's longer, you may lose people's attention – shorter, you won't get enough information across. Start and finish on time. Include the kitchen staff as well. This may be a good time to let servers taste today's specials and have the kitchen staff tell the waitstaff about them. Also take a moment to review anything pertinent from the previous meeting. You may wish to read out customers' letters, praise employees and assess the team's performance. Finally, bear in mind that waitstaff are getting paid for this time, but not tipped, so be sure to not to take advantage of their time. The following is an example of a possible format for a 10-15 minute pre-shift meeting:

- **Preparation.** Before you start, remember the thing that most determines how your meeting will go is your own state of mind. Are you looking at your staff as a group of dedicated people committed to doing a great job, or a bunch of layabouts looking to milk the system? Are you seeking to facilitate and encourage people's best performances, or are you looking to identify and punish people's mistakes? Rest assured that whichever it is, your staff feels it. Your attitude will directly affect their performance. Get committed to build on people's strengths and hold energizing staff meetings.

- **Good news (1-2 minutes).** Acknowledge what works and create a good mood. Find something about the business that shows that your staff is doing a good job and making guests happy. Acknowledge the doer or bearer of the news with sincerity.

- **Daily news (2-3 minutes).** Outline today's specials and upcoming events.

- **Ask your staff (5 minutes).** This is the most important part of the meeting. It provides a great opportunity to find out what's really going on in your restaurant. Listen. Don't interrupt with your own thoughts and don't judge people's comments. Let them share opinions. Create a safe space for open dialog and for learning from one other. How well you listen directly affects how much they're willing to say. Since they are the restaurant, as well as your access to the nitty-gritty, get them talking. If they're shy, ask them questions: What's working for you guys? What's making things tough? Where have things broken down? Which questions from customers have you been unable to answer? Once you get the ball rolling you may find it hard to stop! Good. That means people have things to say and you'll benefit. Asking the rest of the staff if they feel the same way as the speaker is a good way to see if there is a group sentiment and to gauge the size of the issue being presented.

- **Training: the latest news (3–5 minutes).** If staff comments run over, let it cut into this time. It's important that your staff learns from you, but it's more important for you to learn from them. Plus, they will be open to learning from you if they know you're listening to them. Use this time to talk about a single point you want your staff to focus on during this shift, to give out specific knowledge about a product or to train in another targeted way. Focus is important. If you tell people how long the meeting will last and hold to that, they'll give you their attention. If you go over, you'll lose their attention and their trust.

Documenting Personnel and Company Policies

Federal law mandates that all employers, regardless of size, must have written policy guidelines. Employee handbooks/policy manuals are used to familiarize new employees with company policies and procedures. They also serve as guides for personnel management. Formally writing down your policies could keep you out of court, prevent problems and misunderstandings, save time spent answering common questions, and look more professional to your employees. Explaining and documenting company policy to your employees has been proven to increase productivity, compliance and retention. Here are some guidelines:

- **Standard employee handbook guide.** If you have ever written a policy document before, you know how time-consuming it can be. Even if you were a lawyer, it could easily take you 40 hours to research and write a comprehensive employee manual. To pay someone to draw one up for you can cost thousands of dollars. Atlantic Publishing has put together a standard employee handbook guide for the food service industry. All you have to do is edit the information. The template contains all of the most important company handbook sections and it's written in Microsoft Word so that customizing and printing your manual will be as easy as possible. The program currently sells for around $70 and is available at www.atlantic-pub.com, 800-541-1336; Item EHB-CS.

- **Legal disputes.** Lack of communication, along with inadequate policies and guidelines, have been cited as major factors in workplace legal disputes. Failure to inform or notify employees of standard policies has resulted in the loss of millions of dollars in legal judgments. Simply not being aware that their actions violated company policy has been an effective defense for many terminated employees. Most important is to have the employee sign a document stating he or she has received, reviewed, understands and intends to comply with all policies in the manual.

CHAPTER SIX

TRAINING TOPICS

Carrying Trays

Carrying trays is a large part of your servers' job and there are right and wrong ways to go about it. If you have ever been on the other end of a tray of food sliding to the floor, you know that! When servers are hoisting that tray up, be sure they remember that entrées and beverages should be served from the right and side dishes from the left:

- **Food trays.** If your server is carrying a large tray, he or she should set it down on a tray jack to serve. It is easy enough to serve from a small tray, but serving becomes a hazard if waitstaff tries to hold a heavy tray and serve from it. Another option, if another server is not busy, is to have a second server tail the first one and hold the tray while the original waitperson serves from it.

- **Loading trays.** Load food trays with the heaviest entrée nearest to your body so that you can use your body to help balance. Also be sure your servers are balancing the entrées on the tray. Plates that are going out to the dining room for service should never be stacked; if the server needs two trays, have them use two trays.

- **Cocktail trays.** Cocktail trays should be loaded with the heaviest drink in the center to balance the tray. Handles should face outward so that the server can easily grasp the cup or glass.

- **Arm service.** Many servers carry food or drinks without trays. This should only be done for small parties so that all the food can go out at once. If the party is large enough to require two trips using arm service, the server should use a tray. Servers should be able to carry four plates (three on the right hand and arm and one on the left), or three glasses or two cups and saucers.

- **Bussing.** When using trays for bussing, make sure that your servers stack "like" plates in neat stacks. They should do this as quietly as possible in the dining room. Furthermore, don't let your serving staff scrape the plates while still in the dining room. This is unappetizing and can easily be done in the back.

Taking Orders

Before a new employee is allowed to wait at table, make sure he/she knows how to take an order. This information can easily be taught with role playing exercises or by shadowing. Before the servers are let loose on the floor, you may want to consider having them wait on you as a "final exam". This way you'll be certain they're taking orders properly! Here are some useful guidelines:

- **Approaching the table.** The server should approach a table within the first minute of people being seating. This is the first impression your servers will make on your guests. Make sure they look professional and neat. Shirts should be tucked in and ironed and aprons should be clean. The server should smile, make eye contact, and greet the customers giving the customers his or her name. The server or a busser or the host should also bring water to the table during or before this exchange.

- **Taking a drinks order.** When the server approaches the table for the first time, he/she should ask if anyone would like a drink. The server may want to make a suggestion or simply provide the customers with some information on what types of soft drinks or beers the restaurant carries. Be sure your servers know their drink jargon for this exchange. The guest that orders a vodka martini up with a twist will be miffed if he or she receives a gin martini on the rocks! This is also a good time to tell the table about any specials.

- **Serving the drinks.** Drinks should be served quickly. Make sure your servers put cocktail napkins under drink glasses. At this point, the server can ask if they are ready to order. If the table isn't ready, the server should check back with them within a reasonable amount of time. Tell your servers to look for clues that the table is ready. The most obvious clue is that everyone has closed the menus.

- **Taking the food order.** Normal etiquette dictates that you start with the women at the table. If there are children it is also appropriate to start with them. Again, take clues from the table. If one woman is obviously undecided you may make her uncomfortable by insisting she places her order, first. Let the others order, then come back to her.

Make sure your servers have a thorough knowledge of the menu and can answer any questions about menu item preparation. They may also make recommendations at this point, if the customer asks or seems unsure.

- **Delivering the food.** Make sure your servers know that food is served from the right side of the guest and plates are cleared from the right. Also, be sure that when your servers hold plates that they are only touching them on the edge. It's quite unappealing to see your server's thumb in your mashed potatoes! Additionally, servers should bring everyone's food at the same time. Make sure that they caution guests when plates are hot.

- **Checking back.** Be sure servers check back with guests within the first 2-3 minutes of being served. If there is a problem, the server will be able to take care of it immediately. Don't let the customer sit stewing and growing madder about a mistake.

- **Dessert.** When the server is clearing the entrée plates or not long after, he or she should ask if the table wants desserts, coffees or after-dinner drinks. You may want to supply servers with dessert menus or a dessert tray to show the customers. They could also make suggestions for desserts to split, if everyone is feeling quite full. Often a table will split a dessert, and one sale is better than none!

- **The check.** When it looks obvious that the table is getting ready to go or when the customer asks for the check, the server should bring it promptly. It's also a good idea for the server to explain the restaurant's payment procedures. He or she could say, "When you're ready, I'll come back to take care of that for you."

- **Good-byes.** It's a nice touch for the server to say goodbye as the party is leaving. It leaves the customer with a friendly feeling. After all, they've just spent an hour or so in the company of your server!

- **Serving multiple tables.** Once your servers master how to wait on one table, they need to learn how to wait on multiple tables. Let's say a server is responsible for three tables. The first two tables are seated at the same time. The server brings water to both of these tables. Then the server should take a drinks order from each table. By the time the server returns with the drinks, the host has seated the third table. The server should stay with the first two tables and see if they're ready to order. If they are, the server should then take the order, swing by and get a drink order from Table 3. Next, he or she should take the food order from Tables 1 and 2 to the kitchen. After the server drops this off, he or she will return with Table 3's beverages and see if they are ready to order. If you see that a server is in the woods, help the server or get the host/hostess or a busser to help. Also try to limit the number of tables a server is responsible for to four or five. Beyond that, excellent service becomes impossible.

Electronic Ordering Systems

In recent years many restaurants have switched to an "Electronic Guest Check System" or "Wireless Waiter." These systems use a mobile computer. The waitperson carries the mobile computer pad and places the order on the touch-screen display. As each dish is entered, this information is transferred, in real time, to the kitchen, where the order is printed out. The drink order is taken first and sent to the bar. The mobile computer is carried by the server. He or she is then notified by a beep or vibration when the order is ready for pickup, or a "runner" delivers the meal. The "Wireless Waiter" has many advantages including:

- **Less distance to travel for the servers.** Using a "Wireless Waiter," the waitstaff can place multiple orders, without ever walking into the kitchen or bar to check for previously placed orders or to pick up prepared orders.

- **Visibility.** The waitstaff can always keep the customers within their field of vision.

- **The bill is calculated automatically,** removing the risk of human error.

- **Ease of processing credit cards.** Most systems have an optional snap-on credit card reader, which can be attached to the bottom of the handheld device. Customer credit cards are swiped through the handheld unit and processed. Under this system, customers can feel confident that their credit cards are safe, as they are never out of sight.

- **Better service.** Because waitstaff are always visible in the dining area, customers are able to attract their waitperson's attention easily. In addition, servers can wait on six or seven tables at a time – twice as many tables as before. If more tables are waited upon, more tables can be turned, providing the opportunity to increase sales volume.

- **Reduced labor costs.** Utilizing this system, you might need fewer waitpersons, since each one will be able to handle more customers. This would, of course, result in a reduction of labor costs.

Reducing Waste

Cutting costs and raising sales are great ways to increase your bottom line, but one of the hidden areas that may be sucking profits down the drain is waste. While your kitchen staff has an enormous impact on waste, your serving staff can help cut waste, as well. The three main areas where servers can have an impact upon waste are breakage, throwing out unused sugar packets, cracker packs, jellies, etc., and throwing out silverware or linen. Here's how to reduce wastage:

- **Trap the silverware.** Buy a magnetic trap for your garbage cans to catch silverware that is accidentally thrown away. See www.atlantic-pub.com.

- **Waste basket.** Set up a waste basket specifically for broken dishes. This will show your servers the volume of waste that accumulates. You may also want to post the costs of replacing dinnerware, silverware and linen, so the serving staff can see how expensive it is to replace these items.

- **Proper techniques.** Train your serving staff the proper way to load a bus pan to prevent breakage.

- **Incentives.** Provide incentives for your servers to cut back on waste. You could offer a bonus to the shift that has the least waste in a month or give a gift certificate to the employee that comes up with the best cost-saving measure each month.

How to Handle Complaints

No matter how much you strive for perfection, you will get customer complaints in your food service operation. How you handle those complaints determines whether or not you alienate the customer or turn them into repeat business. Your servers, who are always on the front line, have an enormous impact on determining this. Here are a few golden rules for handling complaints:

- **The customer is always right.** Remember, the customer is always right. Make sure this becomes a mantra for your servers. The customer is paying the bill and we, as restaurant employees and managers, should do everything in our power to see that the guest's experience is positive.

- **Apologize.** Before anything else happens, you and/or the server should offer a sincere apology for the mistake and offer to fix it.

- **Respond quickly.** By responding to a problem quickly, you prevent it from becoming a crisis. If a wrong order goes out of the kitchen, fix it immediately; don't make the guest wait in line for his correct meal.

- **Listen.** Make sure you listen to your customer's complaint. Show the guest that you are concerned and sincere in offering your apology. Do something to show that that customer's business is important to you.

- **Compensation.** There are many ways to compensate a customer for a mistake. Taking something off the bill or offering free dessert or a round of drinks are popular methods. If something is spilled on a guest, you should offer to pay the dry cleaning bill. You could also give the guest a free gift certificate for their next meal or send flowers to their workplace or residence.

- **Set guidelines.** Set guidelines for what the server can do to correct a problem. It's annoying for the customer and the server to have to track the manager down to correct a problem. If a customer's soup is cold, the server should be able to say, "Can I bring you another cocktail while I get you another bowl? It's on the house." It's irritating and reflects poorly on management if the server has to say, "Let me check with the manager, maybe we can take something off your bill." By not giving your servers some power in these situations, it tells them that you don't trust them. It also tells the customer that the restaurant cares more about finances than the customer's experience.

- **Give servers a support mechanism.** Even though the customer is always right, make sure your servers know you support them. Don't let your server stand there and say, "No, I'm afraid the chef can't prepare the dish that way," then have a manager step over and say, "Of course the chef can do that." Give your servers consistent dining room rules to follow and make sure you follow them as well!

- **Phone complaints.** If a customer calls with a complaint, do not keep the customer waiting on hold. Write down the caller's name, address and phone number and respond to the compliant in a soothing, courteous tone. Apologize for the problem and offer a solution. Managers should also follow up on the complaint by calling back in a day or so to be certain the situation was handled satisfactorily.

Restaurant Policies

All of your employees should be trained regarding your specific restaurant policies. Make sure employees get written versions of these policies and that you all follow the rules laid down by government policies. Reinforce their learning by including information on policies in regular training meetings. Some policies, including EEO, sexual harassment and ADA, are required by law. Focus on the following:

- **A good general resource for policies is HR Laws Index.** Log on to www.hrlawindex.com/index.html.

- **Equal Employment Opportunity (EEO).** The Federal Equal Employment Opportunity Act requires employers to treat all employees in a fair, non-biased manner, in all aspects of hiring, training, promotion and development.

- **Americans with Disabilities Act (ADA).** This act, passed in Congress in 1990, prohibits employers from discriminating against individuals with mental or physical handicaps, or the chronically ill. The Equal Employment Opportunity Commission (EEOC) offers free workshops about tax incentives for small businesses that hire individuals with disabilities. For more information on the workshops, visit www.eeoc.gov/initiatives/nfi/index.html.

- **Sexual harassment.** Sexual harassment is an ugly fact of life. Make your employees aware that it won't be tolerated in your establishment. Have a written sexual harassment policy in place and be sure that each employee receives a copy. Go a step further and require each new employee to receive training on the topic. There are many videos available for such training from various sources. Log on to www.trainingabc.com/hotel.htm for videos specific to the restaurant industry. The Sexual Harassment Training Video Series Web site is another source for training materials. It can be found at www.sexualharassmentvideos.com. You can find more specific information on the EEOC's guidelines on sexual harassment at www.eeoc.gov. In addition, the EEOC offers training and free publications on the subject of sexual harassment.

- **Discipline.** Every workplace should have a written disciplinary procedure in place, with written copies of this procedure for each employee. Enforce the policy at all times. It's bad for morale if you have an employee that constantly gets away with inappropriate behavior. It can save yourself a lot of headaches when it comes to a former employee suing you for wrongful termination. Make sure to document reports of all disciplinary action and put such reports in employee files. Determine what types of behavior require discipline in your restaurant. A server being late one time probably does not fall into this category. Chronic absenteeism, theft, drinking on the job and substandard work are legitimate reasons to begin the disciplinary process. Review your policy with employees annually.

- **Pay.** Make sure your staff knows your pay policies. These should be communicated to all new hires and included in orientation packets.

Safety

Workplace accidents happen. How you respond to them can make all the difference between life and death. The first thing to do is to have a safety plan in place and train your servers to know and understand the elements of this plan so that they can respond calmly and quickly. If you live in an area that experiences tornado activity, include what to do in the event. All plans should include fire diagrams. You should also have a posted fire egress route, fire extinguishers and first-aid kits on the premises. Here are some good ways to train your servers (and the rest of the staff) on safety issues:

- **Red Cross.** Offer your staff Red Cross training. Make sure all of your servers know universal precautions, first aid, the Heimlich Maneuver and CPR. Contact the Red Cross at www.redcross.og.

- **Fire department.** Your local fire department will give your employees free training on how to use fire extinguishers.

- **Drills.** Put your employees through fire and tornado drills. If an incident occurs, it will be up to your employees to help your customers out, so make sure they know what to do. You can also engage in first-aid drills during training meetings. Have one employee fake an illness or injury and see how appropriately and quickly another employee responds.

- **OSHA.** The Occupational Safety and Health Agency

(OSHA) is the federal agency that oversees safety in the workplace. Make sure you are in compliance with all their regulations. To find out more about their requirements for food service establishments, visit them online at www.osha.gov.

Tips-Reporting Policies

Be sure to advise all new hires about your tip-reporting procedures. Have this procedure in written form and review it annually. Consider the following issues:

- **Who has to report tips?** Employees who receive $20 or more in tips per month are required to report their tips to you in writing. When you receive the tip report from your employee, you should use it to figure the amount of Social Security, Medicare and income taxes to withhold for the pay period on both wages and reported tips. For more information on employer tip reporting responsibilities, visit the IRS's Web site at www.irs.gov and look at Publication 15, Circular E, Employer's Tax Guide. For more information on employee responsibilities, look at Publication 531, Reporting Tip Income.

- **Recent Supreme Court ruling.** In June 2002, the Supreme Court ruled that the IRS can estimate a restaurant's aggregate tip income and bill the restaurant owner for its share of Social Security and Medicare taxes on unreported tips. This ruling puts a greater burden on restaurateurs to make sure employees declare all tip income, because it is likely they will be overcharged by the IRS if they incorrectly estimate the tips earned. Because this ruling is so recent, it is unclear exactly how it will affect tip-reporting procedures for restaurant owners. Currently, the laws are not affected by the court's recent ruling and employees are still legally responsible for reporting all tips to their employers once a month. In turn, employers are still responsible for reporting these amounts to the IRS and paying the FICA tax on the amount.

- **Tip Reporting Alternative Commitment (TRAC).** Many restaurant legal experts suggest that in the current climate, if you don't have a TRAC agreement with the IRS, you should consider entering into one. Under a TRAC agreement, the restaurant says that it will educate employees about tip-reporting requirements and maintain and file tip-related paperwork. In return, the IRS agrees not to pursue restaurant owners for their share of payroll taxes on unreported tips. A TRAC agreement won't protect you from a full audit, but it may help your situation.

- **How to train your servers about tip reporting.** Include this information in your orientation packets for new hires. You also may want to purchase a tip-reporting kit from www.restaurant-workshop.com. These kits include educational materials that you can distribute to your servers. Also consider inviting an accountant to do a training session with your servers.

- **Restaurant industry action.** The National Restaurant Association is lobbying Congress to ask that they clearly state that the IRS cannot use the aggregate assessment method to pressure employers to police tipped employees as to their tipped income. Obviously, this matter is not completely settled. To keep current with information related to IRS rules on tip reporting, log on to the IRS's Web site at www.irs.gov and the National Restaurant Association's Web site at www.restaurant.org.

- **Resources.** The Tip Reporting Education Kit from the National Restaurant Association includes posters, payroll-stuffers, manager checklists and employee brochures to help you convey the tip-reporting laws to your employees. The National Restaurant Association also offers "Legal Problem Solver for Restaurant Operators," which can be purchased on their Web site at www.restautant.org.

Alcohol Sales Policies

Alcohol sales can be a large source of revenue and a profit maker if a restaurant has a wine and beer or liquor license. Unfortunately, in the current atmosphere it can also be a liability. In recent years, the newspapers have been full of stories about restaurants and/or employees being sued because a patron was driving in a drunken state and hurt or killed someone on the way home. The first step in responsible alcohol sales is to be sure that you and your servers know the laws and the ramifications of the laws that affect alcohol sales. Here are the essentials:

- **Have an alcohol sales policy in place.** This policy should include a description of federal, state and local laws that govern your alcohol sales. It should also lay down a set of rules for your servers, including not selling to minors and not selling to intoxicated customers. You should also set limits. For example, put a policy into place that says if a customer has four drinks, the server should notify the manager. The manager can then monitor the situation and determine whether or not the customer needs to be cut off. You may also want to set up a relationship with a local cab company for those occasions when you need to suggest a cab to one of your patrons.

- **Train your servers.** Make sure your servers know and follow your alcohol sales policies. Tell them to keep track of customers' intake if it looks like there may be a potential problems. You can also have them offer a menu to a customer who may only be drinking. If necessary, you may want to bring an intoxicated patron a freebie. In the long run, this is much cheaper than a lawsuit! Also, be sure that servers are checking IDs and your bartenders are measuring the amount of alcohol they are pouring. Role playing exercises and videos are good training methods to use for alcohol sales. Have one server play an intoxicated customer and the other take the role of server. How does each employee handle the situation? Have a group discussion after the exercise.

- **If an incident happens.** Make sure your server gets management involved in any incident. Also, document everything that occurs.

- **Resources.** The National Restaurant Association Educational Foundation offers training materials related to responsible beverage-alcohol service. You can find this information at www.nraef.org. The Web site www.restaurantbeast.com offers free downloads of an alcohol awareness brochure, an alcohol awareness test for servers, a blood alcohol concentration (BAC) guide and a state BAC reference. You can also find information about alcohol abuse at the International Center for Alcohol Policies' Web site, www.icap.org.

How to Serve Alcohol

While your servers don't need to understand the distilling or fermenting processes, they should be familiar with different types of alcohol, different glasses and the basic terminology:

- **Serving.** Waitstaff should always serve alcoholic beverages promptly. How quickly someone gets their drink can set the tone and mood for the customer that evening. If the server does not arrive with the drink for 10 minutes, the customer realizes his or her meal service will probably be equally slow. If the server is backed up, a hostess/host or manager should step in and see that the table receives its drinks quickly. As with food, women are generally served first.

- **Glassware.** Different glasses are used for different alcohol beverages. Make sure your servers know the difference between a jigger, highball glass, martini glass and champagne flute, as well as the difference between red and white wine glasses. Make sure your servers always pick up glassware correctly. They should never touch the rim; glasses should be picked up by the handle or the base in the case of a wine glass.

- **Types of alcohol.** In addition to knowing glassware, your server should be familiar with the different types of alcohol. For example, make sure your waitstaff knows that whiskey can refer to

Irish whiskey, bourbon, rye, scotch, blended and Canadian.

- **Testing their knowledge.** Test your servers' knowledge of alcohol and alcohol service. Make the test fun, however, by awarding a prize to the server who gets the highest score and the server who improved the most from the last test. Role playing also works well. Have one of your servers act like the customer and order various drinks. Have the second server bring back the appropriate glass and bottle of alcohol. Other games work for testing this knowledge as well. You could set up teams and play a revised version of Family Feud or Jeopardy. For example, if you are going to play Jeopardy, make the categories "How to Mix," "What Not to Say to an Intoxicated Customer," "Blood Alcohol Levels," "Types of Vodka" and "Food and Wine." Make it a team effort and award prizes to the winning team.

Wine

While wine is alcohol, we treat it separately here because there are more nuances to wine service than the service of other alcoholic beverages. Many people enjoy drinking wine with food, so the service of wine involves a greater knowledge of the wine itself than with other alcoholic drinks. If someone orders a scotch and soda for dinner, they don't worry whether it goes with the lamb special. When a guest orders wine, however, they usually try to pair it with the food they are ordering. Because of the important link between food and wine, many restaurants do not take a wine order until after the guests have placed their food orders. The following guidelines will help you serve wine with flair:

- **Bottle sizes.** Most restaurants have 750-milliliter wine bottles for bottle sales. They may also offer splits of wine or champagne, which are generally half the size of a regular bottle. Most restaurants also stock larger bottles of house wines to use for individual glass service.

- **Wine language.** It is important that your servers know the basics about wine, the most common grape varieties and how people discuss wine. Your servers should be able to discuss wines' color, smell ("nose") and taste ("palate"). You may also want them to be able to distinguish more subtle color difference. Is the wine yellow like a Chardonnay or is it clearer like a Pinot Grigio? Some of the terms people use to describe smell and taste include dry, sweet, earthy and smoky. They may also say that a wine's taste is reminiscent of another flavor, such as raspberries or pepper. Most importantly, your servers should know which wines in your establishment are sweet and which are dry. This will be the main category upon which guests will base their wine decisions. For helpful advice about wine language, visit www.demystifying-wine.com.

- **Reading wine labels.** Franklin Miami Publishing's guide *How to Read Wine Labels* summarizes all you need to know about interpreting the information on wine labels. Go to www.franklinmiamipublishing.com.

- **Helping a customer choose wine.** Many customers will look to the server for expert advice on what wine to choose. Make sure your servers are comfortable in this role. To do this, the first thing that must happen is that the servers need to be familiar with the restaurant's wine list and how all the wines taste. If the customer is particularly wine savvy, the server could suggest getting a manager or someone else, with greater wine knowledge, to help the customer. You should also encourage servers to let customers have a taste of the wines that you offer by the glass.

- **Serving wine.** Red wines should be served at room temperature and white wines should be chilled to about 50 degrees. To serve a bottle of wine, present the bottle to the person that ordered it, with the label facing the customer. Once the customer has approved the wine, set the bottle on the corner of the table to open it. Cut the foil off the lower lip of the bottle top and put the foil in your apron pocket. Remove the cork and pour an ounce or two for the person who ordered it to taste. You can also set the cork beside this person so they can inspect it, if they want to. After the customer has tasted and approved the wine, pour the wine for all the guests partaking, starting with the women in the group. When you finish pouring a glass, give the bottle a half turn as you raise it to help keep from making spills. Also keep a napkin next to the bottleneck to catch any spills. When filling wine glasses, the server should fill to one-half or two-thirds.

- **Pronunciation.** Be sure your servers are familiar with how to pronounce all the wines on your wine list.

- **Wine and food.** Your servers should know how to suggest what wine will complement what entrée. You can help them out by including this information on your menu if there is room, but servers still need to know how to make suggestions for your customer.

- **Wine resources.** There are many books and magazines on wine. Some of the more respectable ones include *Exploring Wine: The Culinary Institute of America's Complete Guide to Wines of the World;* Robert Parker's *Buying Guide;* Oz Clarke's *Encyclopedia of Wine;* Hugh Johnson's *Wine Atlas;* Tom Steven's *New Sotheby's Wine Encyclopedia;* and *Hachette Wine Guide 2002.* Recognized as "The French Wine Bible" and "The Definitive Guide to French Wine," this Hachette guide contains over 9,000 wines chosen from 30,000 and described by 900 experts.

- **Online resources.** Try Wine Spectator at www.winespectator.com; Wine and Spirits at www.wineandspiritsmagazine.com; and Wine Enthusiast at www.wineenthusiast.com. There also are Web resources for information on wine. Tasting Wine's site, www.tasting-wine.com/html/etiquette.html is a good resource as is Good Cooking's wine terminology Web page at www.goodcooking.com/winedefs.asp. Finally, the American Institute of Wine and Food's Web site has information on local chapters at www.aiwf.org, and Wines.com at www.wines.com offers expert answers, virtual wine tastings and an online searchable database.

- **Training about wine.** One of the best ways to train your serving staff about wines is to let them taste it! Hold regular wine tastings for your servers. Make wine-tasting cards and have them fill out the cards about the specifics of the wines they are tasting. Many times your wine vendors can be called upon to help with such training.

You should also hold sessions that include tasting menu items so that the servers can understand why a Cabernet Sauvignon is a good choice with a steak, but a better selection with fish maybe a Sauvignon Blanc. You can train servers how to pour wine from the bottle by using empty bottles with colored water.

Food Safety

Every member of your staff should be trained in food safety. Causing a food-borne illness can have a major impact on your sales. Not only do you have the chance of being sued, but many health departments and newspapers publicize food-borne illness incidents, and this is not the kind of advertisement that will bring in customers! In addition, food-borne illness can be potentially life threatening. Older customers, children and those with chronic diseases are particularly vulnerable to serious consequences from food-borne illness. You and your staff will need to know the following basics:

- **Buy and use separate color-coded cutting boards** for all food products to prevent cross-contamination. See www.atlantic-pub.com.

- **Use a sanitizer to clean surfaces that come into contact with food.**

- **Make sure employees frequently wash their hands.**

- **HACCP (Hazard Analysis Critical Control Point).** Until recently, HACCP was almost exclusively used in food production plants, but restaurants are beginning to adopt this approach to food safety. Having a HACCP system in place could save you a fortune in liability costs. If a situation arises, you may be able to prove you were using reasonable care and this can go a long way in a liability suit.

- **There are seven principals HACCP uses.** Basically, these principals say that you need to identify all the critical points at which food can become unsafe, such as during cooking, storage and production. Then you must put measures in place to ensure food remains safe. These measures can include actions such as establishing minimum cooking times for menu items and having policies about how long food can remain at room temperature before it must be thrown away. Additionally, you must establish methods to monitor that these policies are being followed and you must establish corrective actions to take if the safety measures have not been applied. For more information on HACCP, HACCP checklists and HACCP form templates, log on to the Food Safety, Education and Training Alliance's Web site at www.fstea.org/resources/tooltime/forms.html.

- **Salmonella.** Most of us are familiar with salmonella and E. coli, but there are many other food-borne illnesses with a range of similar symptoms. For more information on these illnesses, log on to the Center for Disease Control's Web site at www.cdc.gov/health/default.htm#F and look under the topic "food-borne illness." To train your servers on the various illnesses, use flash cards. Have the illness on one side and what causes it on the other. Then, create a game and see who can get the most flash cards right in a 3-minute period. Award the winner a movie gift certificate!

- **Cross-contamination.** Food-borne illnesses are often caused by cross contamination. This means that the bacteria from one food source crosses to another. While most cross-contamination cases occur in the back-of-the-house, servers can cause this situation as well. An example of this is using the same cutting board to cut salad tomatoes and to slice raw chicken. Keep separate cutting boards for the salad and server areas. There are colored acrylic cutting boards on the market that can serve as a reminder for the board's use. Hang a sign up over the area the cutting boards are stored telling servers that the green ones are for salad ingredients.

- **Unsanitary practices.** Unsanitary practices your servers should avoid include chewing gum, eating food in food preparation areas and tasting food using their fingers. Also, make sure that servers cover any cuts and use gloves when handling food. In addition, encourage your workers to stay home if they are ill. Someone with a cold or the flu should not be handling food. Restaurant workers are notorious for coming to work sick in order to avoid losing money. Encourage your employees to practice food safety by putting policies in place that will encourage them to stay home when ill. Consider providing your employees with sick time. Perhaps you could add it as a benefit after an employee has been with you for a certain length of time. By adding this benefit, you can keep your food supply safer and lower your turnover rate.

- **Training.** There are many ways to train servers about food safety. You can enroll them in the National Restaurant Association's ServSafe program or area colleges. While you can do some in-house training, it's best to get expert training when it comes to something as critical as food safety.

- **Information resources.** There are many food safety information resources on the Web. Log on to the following sites for more information:
  - Food Safety Training and Education Alliance, www.fstea.org offers training materials including videos and brochures.

  - The USDA has training materials available on their Web site as well as HACCP materials,www.nal.usda.gov/fnic/foodborne/haccp/ index.shtml.

  - The Food Safety and Inspection Service of the U.S. Department of Agriculture, www.fsis.usda.gov/OA/consedu.htm, has information and training resources.

  - The American Food Safety's Web site, www.americanfoodsafety.com, offers courses in food safety and Food Protection Manager Certification.

  - The National Restaurant Association's Educational Foundation, www.nraef.org offers ServSafe certification.

  - Food Safety First, www.foodsafetyfirst.com, offers videos you can use for training.

  - Resources on www.restaurantbeast.com provide many downloads pertaining to food safety, including a food-borne illness complaint form checklist for documentation, a food-safety brochure with food-handling facts and recom- mendations, a food-safety quiz, FDA guidelines for HACCP programs and a handwashing sign.

  - Gateway to U.S. Government Food Safety Information, www.foodsafety.gov.

- Bad Bug Book, vm.cfsan.fda.gov/
  ~mow/intro.html.

- Safety Alerts, www.safetyalerts.com.

- E. Coli Food Safety News: MedNews.Net®,
  www.MedNews.Net/bacteria.

- Safe Food Consumer, www.safefood.org.

- Food Safe Program, foodsafe.ucdavis.edu/
  homepage.

- International Food Safety Council,
  www.nraef.org/ifsc/ifsc_about.asp?level1_id=2
  &level2_id=1.

"Are Your Hands Really Clean?"

Handwashing is perhaps the most critical aspect of good personal hygiene in the entire food service. In fact, one of the easiest practices your staff can engage in to avoid food-borne illness and eliminate cross-contamination is washing their hands. In the food industry, your servers' hands come into contact with many potential bacteria-carriers. To wash their hands properly, servers should wash them under warm water with soap for 20 seconds, making sure to scrub between the fingers and up the forearms. After washing, the employee should use a hand sanitizer. Make it easy for your servers to wash their hands throughout their shifts. In addition, when working with food, they should wash gloved hands as often as bare hands. Have a handwashing sink installed near their area and be sure paper towels, soap and sanitizer are available. Also, make sure your employees always wash their hands after smoking a cigarette.

- **Try the following exercise:** First, you'll need a fluorescent substance and a black light. (One possible source for these is Atlantic Publishing's Glo Germ Training Kit. See www.atlantic-pub.com or call 800-541-1336.) Using these materials, you can show trainees the "invisible dirt" that may be hiding on their hands.
  - Have employees dip their hands in the fluorescent substance.

  - Tell employees to wash their hands.

  - Have employees hold their hands under the black light to see how much "dirt" is still there.

  - Explain proper handwashing technique.

  - Have employees wash their hands again, this time using the proper handwashing technique.

  - Have employees once again hold their hands under the black light.

Basic Terminology

Make sure your servers are schooled in basic cooking terminology. Here are some of the more important terms with which they should be familiar:

- **Baked/roasted** – cooked in the oven, uncovered.

- **Blackened** – seasoned with spices including cayenne and cooked over extremely high heat in a heavy skillet.

- **Braised** – cooked in the oven, covered.

- **Coulis** – a thick pureed sauce.

- **Deep fried** – food is submerged in hot, liquid fat and thoroughly cooked.

- **Fried** – cooked in hot fat, usually butter or oil, over medium to high heat.

- **Grilled** – cooked on a grate over charcoal, wood or gas.

- **Marinade** – a liquid used to flavor food before cooking, can include herbs, spices, lemon, oil or alcoholic beverages.

- **Poached** – cooked in or over boiling water.

- **Purée** – ingredient is blended until it reaches a smooth consistency. Many salad dressings and sauces are made with fruit or vegetable purées.

- **Reduce** – to boil a liquid rapidly until evaporation reduces the volume. This intensifies the flavor; it is often a method used for sauces.

- **Roux** – equal parts of flour and fat cooked over high heat. Used to thicken sauces; most commonly used in Cajun cooking.

- **Sautéed** – cooked very quickly in a small amount of fat over direct heat.

- **Seared** – usually refers to meat and means browning quickly by subjecting the item to very high heat.

- **Steamed** – cooked by placing over a rack or in a steamer basket and then placed over simmering or boiling water in a covered pan.

- **Stewed** – the food is barely covered with liquid and simmered slowly in a pan with a tightly fitting lid.

- **Simmered** – food is cooked gently in hot liquid, low enough to keep tiny bubbles breaking on the surface.

- **Stir-fried** – quickly fried food cut into small pieces over high heat while constantly stirring.

Sauces

Your servers should know about the following types of sauces:

- **White sauces** – white sauces include béchamel, cream sauces and mustard sauces; they usually include milk or cream.

- **Brown sauces** – these are made with brown stocks. Examples include bordelaise, diablo and chasseur. These sauces often have wine added and do not include cream or milk.

- **Emulsified sauces** – these sauces include hollandaise sauce. It is a sauce made from two ingredients that usually cannot combine. In the case of hollandaise, these ingredients are eggs and lemon juice.

- **Butter sauces** – butter-based sauces include beurre blanc, beurre rouge and beurre noir. The main ingredient in these sauces is butter, but they can also include vinegar, shallots and lemon juice.

- **Salsa/chutneys** – chutneys are made of fruit, vinegar spices and sugar; they are usually cooked. Salsas are cooked or uncooked and usually consist of tomatoes or fruit with chilis, onion, garlic and various other fresh ingredients.

- **Dessert sauces** – these sauces are often made from fruit purées or they can be chocolate or caramel. Coulis often function as dessert sauces. Saybayon refers to dessert sauces made with wine, egg yolks and sugar.

Computerized Guest Checks

Nowadays, most restaurant owners have computerized registers. You'll need to know about the following:

- **Computerized cash register.** These registers have a number of advantages. It is easy to run reports about anything from how many of each entrée was sold on a shift to daily food costs to the number of employee meals rung up that day. Train your servers to use these registers to their fullest extent. Many companies that sell these units also offer low-priced training.

- **Point-of-sale systems (POS).** These systems go a step beyond the simple computerized stand-alone cash register. These systems link the dining room, kitchen and office. You may opt for a server terminal, which can be used at the servers' station to enter information such as the number of guests and food orders. Many of these systems have a touch-screen that guides the server through the process. There are also handheld order terminals available. Servers carry these units with them and enter the information as they are taking it from the customer. With a POS system, the information is automatically generated for the kitchen. Understanding the numbers collected by a POS system will give the operator more control over inventory, bar revenues, labor scheduling, overtime, customer traffic and service. They also reduce the opportunity to pilfer. Some benefits of using a POS system include:
  - Increases sales and accounting information
  - Custom tracking
  - Reports waitstaff's sales and performance
  - Reports menu-item performance
  - Reports inventory usage
  - Processes credit card purchases
  - Accurate addition on guest checks
  - Prevents incorrect items from being ordered
  - Prevents confusion in the kitchen
  - Reports possible theft of money and inventory
  - Records employee time-keeping
  - Reports menu-sales breakdown for preparation and menu forecasting
  - Reduces time spent walking to kitchen and bar

- **POS enhancements.** Many POS systems have been greatly enhanced to include comprehensive home delivery; guest books; online reservations;

frequent diner modules and fully integrated systems with real-time inventory; integrated caller ID; accounting, labor scheduling, payroll, menu analysis, purchasing and receiving; cash management; and reports. Up-and-coming enhancements and add-ons include improved functionality across the Internet, centralized functionality enabling "alerts" to be issued to managers and voice recognition POS technology. Here are a few POS Web sites for additional information:

- www.squirrelsystems.com
- www.alohaenterprise.com
- www.nextpos.com/english/overtureredirproducts.htm
- www.navitech.com/cat-possystems.asp
- www.datadesignsonline.com/pos2.html
- www.microworks.com
- www.bmccomputers.com
- www.restaurant-pos.com
- www.restaurantpos.com
- www.touch2000.com/touchsystems.htm
- www.tradewindsoftware.com
- www.touchnserve.com
- www.chefsystems.com
- www.radiantsystems.com
- managementsolutions1.com

- **POS – the future.** As the labor market continues to diminish, touch-screens with POS systems will become essential. It has been predicted that in the next few years customers may even place their own orders. Terminals will be simply turned around. During peak seasonal periods, ordering food may be like pumping your own gas; customers will key in their own selections and then slide their credit cards through to pay.

Getting Orders to the Kitchen

In many restaurants, the server takes the order by hand at the table, goes to the cashier, server area or another convenient place to enter the information into the computer. Then, depending upon the sophistication of the system, the order either goes to the cooks via the computer system or the server hands the guest check to the kitchen. The order is then placed on a wheel or rack. Most guest checks have multiple layers and writing areas; train your servers how to correctly write the guest check for your kitchen. For instance, the check may have a heavy copy and a carbon layer on top, which is divided into two areas by a perforation. Your server keeps the heavy copy, writes the entrée order on the large section of the perforated sheet and the appetizer on the smaller area. When the guest check goes into the back, the line cook and the appetizer cook split the sheet. For seamless order processing, try the following suggestions:

- **Guest check shorthand.** Even if you're using a computerized register, your servers may still be writing down orders by hand. If you're using a completely computerized system, you still have abbreviations in place for menu items. Make sure your servers memorize these, and if they are writing them by hand for the cooks, make sure the orders are legible!

- **Examples of abbreviations.** Here is a list of some example abbreviations you can use for menu items. When you develop your own system, be careful of repetition and abbreviations that are too similar:
  - Spag & mt – Spaghetti and meatballs
  - Fett – Fettuccine Alfredo
  - Steak w/ mush – Steak Hoagie with

mushroom sauce
- Chic parm – Chicken Parmigiana
- Tossed BC – Tossed salad with blue cheese dressing
- Ch man – Cheese manicotti
- Burger W Let/tom/on – Hamburger, well done, with lettuce, tomato and onion

- **Guest check control.** You should always have control measures in place for your guest checks. This helps prevent employees from giving away food and drinks. Stress that all food that leaves the kitchen has to have a guest check accompany it whether it is for a customer or an employee.

- **Accountability.** Make your servers responsible for accounting for all of their guest checks, at the end of the night, when they turn these over to the manager on duty. Rather than keeping a stack of guest checks for servers to pick up as they come on duty, have the manager on duty issue guest checks and keep a log of who was issued what. Management can then spot check on a random basis and make sure that the amounts and payment methods entered on the guest check match what the computer says.

- **Have a policy in place for what happens if checks go missing.**

CHAPTER SEVEN

MOTIVATING

Working Environment

People are motivated to work hard for employers who care about them. Create a caring work environment and your employees will take the extra effort to make your establishment a better place:

- **Take and use employee suggestions.** Give your staff a support system so that they know you are behind them.

- **Act.** A sure way to develop a poor attitude in staff is to retain someone who is not performing up to standards. Work to train the employee. If the individual is still not making the grade, take action to fire them. Not only is it necessary from a customer service stand point, but it also shows your staff that you are serious about keeping a strong team environment.

- **Ask them.** People buy into an idea a lot easier if they had some input into the idea in the first place. Ask your servers how to generate sales. If you want to increase your appetizer sales, bring everyone together and tell the servers you want to generate more appetizer sales. Let them brainstorm to come up with methods to do this. Then, as a group, pick the top two or three methods and have the servers try these out.

- **Guard against complacency.** It's easy to lose your edge during lulls in business. Find ways to keep servers occupied during this time so they don't lose their momentum. There are always tasks that need to be done, such as rolling silverware or restocking condiments, but try to add some interesting tasks to this down time as well. Let the servers spend some time testing each other on their wine knowledge. They can use flash cards while they wait for business to pick up. You could orchestrate a menu tasting during this time as well. Use it as a testing device as well. Have your servers taste a dish and let each describe it. Give the best description a prize, such as free dinner that night.

- **Benefits.** In an effort to professionalize service, some restaurants pay regular wages every two weeks, with benefits including health and dental insurance, 401(k) plans (with 25-percent matching contributions), paid vacations and merit-based raises. Having these additional benefits will motivate your servers to do a good job. This also promotes longevity. Although it may not be as attractive for the student who wants to work short shifts or flexible schedules, the more mature employees will be very interested.

Unconventional Motivations

Benefits, raises and a caring environment are tried-and-tested ways to motive employees. Try some creative, inexpensive ways as well:

- **Films.** Use films such as "Apocalypse Now" to show how passions lead to outstanding results.

You can have a night out with the staff. If your restaurant is closed Mondays, hold a screening. Bring popcorn and other snacks and have a discussion about the themes from the movie that you want to discuss afterwards.

- **Trips to farms.** Take your serving staff to an organic farm or local winery to learn about the food or wine. This will help in the food and wine education.

- **Pitch in.** Show your staff no job is too small by doing some of the smallest jobs yourself. Help bus tables on a busy night, or put on an apron and rub elbows with the dishwasher when he falls hopelessly behind.

- **Pat on the back.** Inspiration can come from an action as simple as a pat on the back. Make sure you tell your servers when they do a good job and communicate that you are proud they are a part of your team. The time for this type of feedback is in the moment. Don't wait a week to say "good job."

- **Show respect.** It's simple. People are more likely to work hard for someone who respects them. Give them some responsibility. For instance, instead of making them come to you when someone sends an entrée back, give them some guidelines to work within, then let them handle the situation.

Contests

- **Contests should be of short duration.** Contests that go on for over a month tend see a sharp decline in employee interest. Also, make sure there is a carrot at the end of the contest! **135**

- **Set goals and communicate them in personal terms.** Before you begin a contest, make sure you have set goals. Let's say you want to increase your bar sales by 10 percent. We'll say this means you would have to increase your bar sales by 600 drinks per month. Don't tell your servers you want to sell 600 more drinks a month; make the goal more personal and more attainable. Determine how many additional drinks you need to sell each shift to reach this goal. With this information in hand, approach your serving staff and tell them you would like to increase your bar sales by, let's say, 15 drinks per evening. Then, go on to explain how they can help reach this goal.

- **Involve employees as a team.** Include other staff members in the contest as well. If you're focusing on appetizers, for instance, you could reward the kitchen staff according to how many appetizer plates they got out in 5 minutes or less.

- **Have more than one winner.** While competition is healthy, it can also create a stressful environment. Make sure you reward people for improvement as well as for the highest quotas. Generate prizes for those servers who are reaching new personal bests.

- **Who's got the $10 bill?** Try this contest to increase sales during service: Take a $10 bill out of the cash register and tell your servers you want them to sell desserts (or appetizers or glasses of wine) that night. The first person who sells one gets the money. The first to sell two then takes the $10 from the first server. Continue this through the shift. At the end of the shift, the last person with the $10 gets to keep it. You can keep this contest going over several shifts by posting the results on an employee bulletin board.

- **Conduct a raffle.** Another fun way to motivate servers to sell is to hold a raffle. Pick a menu item for which you'd like to increase sales. Tell the servers that each time they sell one, they will get their name dropped into a bowl for the drawing. At the end of the shift, draw for a prize.

- **Tips contest.** This is a great way to motivate your serving staff! Tell your servers that whoever ends up with the most credit card slips at the end of the night with 20 percent in tips, wins a prize.

- **Good employee poker.** A more general contest involves a deck of cards and the best poker hand. At the beginning of the week tell your servers that each time you spot an example of good service, good salesmanship, safety attention or waste watching, you will give that employee a card. At the end of the week the employee with the best poker hand wins a prize.

Feedback

- **Testing.** During the training sessions, give your servers tests. While testing is not the only form of feedback available, it does help the servers measure things such as food-safety knowledge, wine knowledge and menu knowledge.

- **Mystery spotters.** Many restaurants hire people to dine anonymously at their establishments and then report back to management on the service they've received. These individuals can tell you how the food was presented, how they found the service and how long they had to wait to be seated.

- **Comment cards.** Provide your guests with comment cards and share these comments with your staff.

Performance Reviews

Performance reviews are an important way to give your servers feedback on how they're doing. Remember, however, that nothing you say in a review should come as a surprise to your server. Always give your staff regular feedback, both positive and negative. Evaluating and motivating your staff should be a daily task. Consider the following aspects of conducting performance reviews:

- **Intent of reviews.** The results of performance reviews are two-fold. First, the supervisor must use a review in order to judge how well the employee is doing his or her job and whether or not the employee is eligible for a wage increase. Additionally, and perhaps more importantly, reviews are used to set goals for employees.

- **Setting performance review goals.** When setting goals, be sure to make them concrete. Give the server a quantifiable way of reaching his or her goal.

- **Types of review.** In general, there are two kinds of performance reviews. One uses input just from the employee's supervisor. The other type uses input from other staff members as well. Many companies have recently switched to a performance review system that involves other staff members. This type of review, called "360-degree feedback," involves the supervisor collecting information from staff members who work with the employee. The supervisor then takes this information and his or her assessment of the employee and uses this information during the evaluation interview. At no time are names used, so the other employees can feel comfortable giving honest feedback. The site www.360-degreefeedback.com has specific information pertaining to the 360-degree feedback process. Additional sites with human resources information include the International Association for Human Resources Information at www.ihrim.org; www.business.com/directory/ human_resources/index.asp; and The Society for Human Resource Management at www.shrm.org. You also can download performance appraisal forms and related material at www.performance-appraisal-form.com.

- **Self review.** Before you conduct the review, ask the server to review themselves and to bring this review to the session. This will help you to understand how they see themselves.

- **Be specific.** Don't just tell your server, "You need to improve." Give them specific behaviors you would like to see improved and tell them how to go about making positive changes. If the person is doing great, tell them how as well.

- **Be fair.** It's difficult to review someone, but be as fair and consistent as you possibly can.

- **Maintain a review schedule.** Give your employees annual reviews. You may want to schedule all reviews during a month that is always slow. You could also schedule reviews for employees' anniversary dates. For new employees, schedule a review in the first couple of months to give them immediate feedback on their new job.

- **Review questions.** Some of the behavior you will want to find out about in reviews includes the person's relationship with others, their problem-solving skills, accountability, enthusiasm and team spirit. Structure your questions accordingly. Focus questions on the following areas:
  - Does the employee fulfill his or her job duties?
  - Does the employee assist others with work?
  - Is the employee responsible and punctual?
  - Does the employee use sound judgment in keeping a safe work environment?

- **Use a rating system for the questions.** Be sure to include an area for comments on the form as well; if someone is not performing their duties, you will want specific information on the problem areas.

- **Review location.** A performance review should always be conducted on neutral ground. Don't conduct them in your office; the person you are reviewing is likely to feel threatened. The review should not feel like a disciplinary interview; rather, it should be a dialogue between you and an employee with the goal of making the employee more productive. You may want to conduct the review off-premises or you could go to the dining room. If you conduct the review in the dining room, pick a table rather than a booth and sit beside the person rather than facing them. This body language will help make the review feel non-confrontational. It's also very important that reviews be conducted in private, so if you use the dining room, do so when your establishment is closed and other employees and customers are not in the room.

- **Review.** When you go into a review, the employee should not be blind-sided. If you have been having problems with an employee, the review is not the place he or she first hears about it. If that is the case, you need to look closely at your management practices and your disciplinary policy. Start the review on a positive note, then go into any problem areas and end on a positive note. Summarize results and tell the employee what those results are, then talk about future goals. Come to an agreement about what the goals will be and write the plan down. The employee should also have a chance to make comments on the review. Give the employee some time to reflect, then ask that they make their comments in writing. These comments, as well as the review, should go into the employee's personnel file.

Give Them the Tools to Do Their Job

One of the most frustrating things for employees is to know how to do their jobs, but not be given the tools and equipment needed to do the job. Don't cut costs to the extent that you're impeding your servers from delivering top-notch service. Here's how:

- **Hold briefings by chefs during pre-service meetings.** This will help staff members to grasp the finer points of every dish served. While it is easy to review the menu, this contact with the chef will give servers an opportunity to ask questions.

- **Towels.** Nothing can measure the cost for the customer disgusted by seeing the server wipe a table clean with a dirty towel. Give your servers access to enough towels to keep the dining room clean!

- **Pens and guest checks.** If you're going to control issuing guest checks, make sure you or another manager is available at the beginning of the shift to pass them out to the servers. Also, don't make your servers use their own pens. Have plenty available for them and for the customers. In fact, it may be worth looking into getting pens with your restaurant's name on them.

- **Dishes.** Provide your dining room staff with enough china, flatware and linen. Don't make them roll silverware as tables are being seated. This only reflects poorly on you!

Conclusion: Focus on Making Your Guests Happy

The food service business is about personal connection. Getting connected is the way to delight guests and bring them back. Bringing guests back just one time per month will give you a 15–50-percent increase in sales volume. If you dedicate your energies towards building an establishment where your servers are treated with respect and gratitude, they will treat you and your customers in the same way. Focus on building an environment that is friendly, helpful, informed and welcoming and people will come back again and again. This can happen by taking the weight of sales off your staff's shoulders. Everybody – especially customers – should feel they are on the "same page." Your job is to create a place that people think of first when deciding where to eat and that they tell their friends about it.

INDEX